COME *as* YOU ARE

COME *as* YOU ARE

SAMUEL NORTON

Foreword by Jen Norton

CFI
An imprint of Cedar Fort, Inc.
Springville, Utah

Paperback ISBN 13: 978-1-4621-4639-0
Ebook ISBN 13: 978-1-4621-4660-4

Published by CFI, an imprint of Cedar Fort, Inc.
2373 W. 700 S., Suite 100, Springville, UT 84663
Distributed by Cedar Fort, Inc., www.cedarfort.com

Library of Congress Registration Number: 2023942323

Cover design by Shawnda Craig

Edited and Typeset by Kyle Lund

Printed in the United States of America

10 9 8 7 6 5 4 3 2 1

Printed on acid-free paper

This book is dedicated to Olivia, William, Joshua and Benjamin.
My hope is that you might come unto Jesus Christ
and that culture, which should bring you to His
healing power, doesn't get in your way.

Author's Note

The views expressed in this book have been shaped by wonderful teachers, speakers, and thought-leaders but ultimately belong to the author.

Publisher's Note

Out of respect for the author, British English spelling has been retained, unless directly quoting American Church leaders.

Acknowledgments

To our FSY team of counsellors; we were blessed to serve alongside each of you. Thank you for your inspiring examples of faith and devotion to Christ and His restored gospel. To Iain, Moses, Natasha, and cousin Cat; thank you for your rounds of encouragement, feedback and support. To Adam and Madeline; thank you both for being bold in your builds and challenges. To Team MaBeLeNo; thank you for reassuring me that this was a worthy project. To spiritually evergreen, boomer parents, a rock star aunt, and perfectly imperfect siblings who all love the Saviour in their own way; thank you. Your voices help me sing in the choir and your friendship helps me row in the boat. Finally, to Jen; thank you for helping me find Bishop Cambio all those years ago. He continues to bless our lives.

Contents

Foreword

The Saviour taught: "I say unto you, be one; and if ye are not one ye are not mine."[01] And an ancient prophet taught that we "should look forward . . . having [our] hearts knit together in unity and in love one towards another."[02]

It has been my experience that unity is something we grow into. We learn to be one by striving to mourn with those that mourn, to bear one another's burdens, and to comfort those who stand in need of comfort.[03] When I have felt my burdens lifted by others, the shared experience of our hearts knit together has helped me to find a sense of healing. But it was the feelings of being seen, valued and included in the priorities and care of another that helped me to look forward.

I look forward when I feel deep down in my heart that there is a space for me, when I know that my weakness is validated, my voice is heard and my contribution valued—no matter how small or great. I look forward when I know that I am welcomed and included, when I have role models I identify with, and when I hear my story in the stories of others, and when I don't feel judged or pressured to conform. I look forward when I feel no obstacles in my way to come unto Christ and can trust that He will heal me. As I spend more time in His healing influence, I feel slowly sanctified.

In this way the rising generation are no different.

---

01 Doctrine and Covenants 38:27

02 Mosiah 18:21

03 Mosiah 18:8-9

This book is a valuable resource for leaders, parents, and teachers alike. It serves as a guide to how we can create a more inclusive space at church – more inclusive in how we teach, in what we teach and how we treat one another. It has been my local experience that the resulting space will help motivate a much broader group to come unto Jesus Christ.

During a worldwide youth devotional, President Russell M. Nelson said this to our children:

> You were sent to earth at this precise time, the most crucial time in the history of the world, to help gather Israel. There is nothing happening on this earth right now that is more important than that . . . This is the mission for which you were sent to earth.[04]

In other ways, the rising generation are different.

When they feel safe and reassured, they are bold and fearless. They are radically inclusive and have an extraordinarily refined antenna towards even the most subtle exclusionary mindsets, attitudes and behaviours. They have their own values and a clear understanding of how life can be better. They have a voracious appetite for truth and an infectious love of God. Theirs is the healing Christ and not the high performance Christ. They will champion the underdog, the marginalised, and the downtrodden. Encoded into their DNA is the desire to live the baptismal covenant in ways we can scarcely imagine.

But when church feels unsafe, and when exclusionary mindsets, attitudes and behaviours are allowed to persist, many understandably struggle. In time, the fires of their faith burn less bright. They can become frustrated quickly and may look for truth elsewhere. Moreover, in places where these challenges are more acute, the rising generation may be tempted to quickly cancel the content and the content providers. In these moments of loss, we adults would be wrong to think we don't have a shared responsibility.

---

04 Russell M. Nelson and Wendy W. Nelson, *Hope of Israel*, Worldwide Youth Devotional, Conference Center, Salt Lake City, June 2018. https://www.churchofjesuschrist.org/study/broadcasts/worldwide-devotional-for-young-adults/2018/06/hope-of-israel?lang=eng#title1

As their parents, leaders and teachers, part of our role is to help create a safe and inclusive space at church and in our homes for them to come unto Christ, in their way and in His way.

We can listen to them, hear their stories, reassure them, empower and follow them.

With more space, and more safe space, they will find the confidence to do what they were sent here to do—to gather Israel and to help us all look forward.

May this exploration of inclusion inspire you and your loved ones. In our shared journey of faith, may we all come closer to the divine purpose God has for each of us.

Jen Norton

Inclusion is not bringing people into what already exists; it is making a new space, a better space for everyone.

Dr. George Dei[01]

01 G.S.N Dei, *Meeting Equity Fair and Square*, Leadership Conference of the Elementary Teachers' Federation of Ontario, Keynote address, Mississauga, Ontario September 28th, 2006.

Jesus as a Young Adult by Mark Manning

Artist's note: I wanted to draw Christ as a young adult smiling. There is nothing we know about these years so I wanted to show a potential image of him during that time as I teach young adults.

Introduction

MANY YEARS AGO, WHILST SERVING IN A STAKE PRESIDENCY, I ATtended our mid-week presidency meeting and received training from a visitor. In so many ways, what I experienced that night became the catalyst for this book.

Towards the end of the meeting, the visitor asked our stake president what he described as an "important question, that might require some reflection." He leaned in, as though sharing a secret, and with a sincere tone asked: "*How many members of your stake do you think will eventually make it to the Celestial Kingdom?*" Before our stake president could respond, the visitor continued "I always ask this question of stake presidents and I am often dismayed by their answers. One stake president once confided in me that he thought it was as low as fifty and another as low as twenty. We really must be asking more of people."

The visitor, a loving and respectful man, had great faith in Jesus Christ. His sincere intention was, no doubt, to ask a thought-provoking question to support our personal growth as a stake presidency.

Yet, I felt concerned about how many times this conversation had been repeated in other meetings and what its impact might have been on faithful members of the Church—especially our young people. Although I could understand the premise of his question and acknowledged the importance of focusing on exaltation, the conversation troubled me. I felt it judged the members of our stake (both the attending and the wandering) with one broad and dismissive brush and removed all the space from their personal journeys to Christ. Above all, I felt it misrepresented the nature of a loving, concerned God whose work and glory is to bring us all safely home.

As I listened to our visitor talk about his conversations with other local leaders, leaders responsible to not only safeguard the doctrine but to also create safe and reassuring space for people within their respective faith communities, I grew more restless. In what felt like a long time, but which must have been less than a minute, questions came into my mind: "Why is this question being asked? Has anybody ever challenged its premise? Who else thinks like this? Why don't I think like this? What will happen if I challenge the premise? Is it even my place to do so?"

Into my mind came the faces of my friends, past and present ward and stake members, youth and young adults, married and single, so many who struggled and continued to struggle to find their space. "Who is going to stand up for these incredible people?" As my mind raced, I found myself beginning to speak.

As he drew his thoughts to a close, I respectfully said, addressing him by name, "Please ask me your question." A little startled, he agreed:

"President Norton, how many members of this stake do you think will eventually make it to the celestial kingdom?"

With as much quiet dignity as I could muster, I steadied myself, looked him in the eye and summarised my own faith journey to Christ in three small words: *"All of them."*

Thereafter, the tone of the meeting changed, and a discussion began about the plan of an inclusive Father in Heaven, the rescuing condescension of our loving Saviour, the need to be more generous within our local traditions, the need to teach these plain and precious truths with less judgment, and how we could be creating more space for one another to come unto Christ. I remember the exchange as though it were yesterday. I will always be grateful for what it taught me.

For me, the story illustrates a way of thinking that has made it difficult for some of our young people to feel motivated in their faith. I hope we can change that.

I hope we can encourage local adult leaders, teachers, and parents to consider how they can create more space within our local faith traditions for our children to find their personal paths to Christ, so that His love and healing mercy might become powerful influences in their lives.

I hope we can support parents as they embrace more fully a home-centred, Church-supported approach to gospel living, where clear *dos and don'ts* have been replaced in the youth and young adult experience.

I hope we can include all members of the Church.

Creating space will hopefully mean different things to different people. For some leaders, it might mean helping our young people feel validated in their starting points and circumstances. For some parents, it might mean helping our young people express themselves more authentically. For some of our teachers, it might mean creating an environment where they can enjoy more personal experiences with God.

For me, *creating space* means to reassure our young people that being perfected in Him is the eventual destination of their faith and not the entry point. Becoming perfected in Him is translated from the Greek word: *telos,* meaning *made whole* or *complete.* We will be made whole by Him long after our mortal mission is over, long after overcoming the world through His Atonement and after overcoming death through His Resurrection. There's a lot of time (and space) between now and then to learn to love God and to love one another.

Perhaps for some, the idea of giving our young people more space might be scary, especially where we have over-relied upon standardisations that emphasised a singular image of righteousness. For some of us, it might be revealing to explore whether our approach to leading, teaching, and parenting has been founded upon easy-to-follow easy-to-enforce rules, or whether we were helping loved ones truly learn to love God.

If we are to create a more reassuring space for the rising generation to come unto Christ, we will need to challenge certain cultural narratives, attitudes, and behaviours that have become entangled with the doctrine of Christ. Some of these dominant attitudes and behaviours are so tightly held in common (like those expressed in the training meeting exchange) that some might consider it heresy to challenge them.

Entangled narratives can convince the rising generation that their spiritual ambition should be to grow up to be a good Church member, where the local expectations of the few often define the experience of the many. But if we can transform our local traditions to create space for people's personal growth as disciples of Jesus Christ, I believe the rising generation will find greater purpose, fulfilment, and joy that will sustain them, not just throughout their youth experience, but throughout their adult lives.

By letting go of things that matter less – even things that we have held dear and which may have defined our past – more of our young people will find the space they need to come as they are, the space to find their path, the space to be themselves, and the space to express themselves with authenticity. They will find more space to think and feel, more space to engage, more space to speak and be heard, more space to learn (and make mistakes), more space to form and share opinions, and more space to feel validated. They will find more space to hope, more space to believe, more space to learn to trust God, and more space to love Him and seek His healing.

To use an analogy, if their personal faith were a sea-worthy vessel, perhaps a super tanker or even a small rowing boat, entangled cultural narratives, attitudes, and behaviours might be the barnacles on the bow. These barnacles start small and, at first, are perhaps unnoticeable. Once built up, however, they can create friction and increase drag, thereby reducing the boat's travelling speed. The journey becomes inefficient and laboured. The toil eventually becomes too much to bear. The scenery doesn't move in line with expectations, and some may feel that in the face of a choice between being 'all-in' or 'all-out,' they eventually have no other option but to jump overboard.

In 2014, Elder M. Russell Ballard of the Quorum of the Twelve Apostles taught everybody to "stay in the boat" and "hold on."[01] He offered prophetic counsel and advice to "wear a life jacket," to "hold

01 M. Russell Ballard, *Stay in the Boat and Hold On!,* General Conference (Salt Lake City: The Church of Jesus Christ of Latter-day Saints, October 2014), Gospel Library App.

on with both hands," and to "avoid distractions." Building on his analogy, by scraping off the barnacles, by illuminating the inclusive doctrine of Christ, and by helping our young people find their place and feel valued aboard the "Old Ship Zion," I believe many more will have a healing experience and will travel with more authenticity, more vulnerability, more curiosity, more validation, more hope, and more joy.

Although we are making progress as a people, with clear efforts being made to establish a greater focus on all members of The Church of Jesus Christ of Latter-Day Saints personally coming unto Christ, I believe there is more we can do.

As a greater understanding of core doctrine, principle-based teaching, and a more open validation for members finding their own ways to express their faith takes hold, I feel excited to worship in a renewed and more mature environment, motivated by love—one with less judgement, fewer arbitrary rules, less pressure, less fear, and less compulsion. Teaching correct principles and allowing people to govern themselves[02] was a foundational concept in the early days of the Restoration. Returning to this mindset is both exciting and essential.

Because of a renewed focus on Christ, our language is already becoming more inclusive. Agency is being more conspicuously emphasised, as programmes are made more principles-based and organisational structures simplified. It will no doubt take more time for the local experience to adjust. What is clear though is that if the rising generation align with the doctrines of Christ and choose to come unto Him, their radically inclusive approach to accepting others could lead us to an exciting place. We can all make more space for them so that they can help get us there sooner. We can trust them and let them show us the way. Echoing the words of John the Baptist "[they] must increase, but [we] must decrease."[03]

Each chapter in this book opens with a thought, a concern or a question shared by a member of the rising generation. In each case, the name of the individual has been changed. Perhaps notably, each of their concerns is a different way of saying the same thing: *"I'm strug-*

02 James R. Clark, *Messages of the First Presidency*, Volume 3 (Salt Lake City: Bookcraft, 1966), 54.

03 John 3:30

gling to find the space and reassurance I need to find my way to Jesus Christ."

Each chapter explores how space can sometimes be removed and what we can do to restore it. To assist the reader, chapter summaries have also been included by way of a short problem statement and possible response. Each chapter turns to core doctrine, scripture, prophetic quotes, and faith-filled anecdotes – many of which come from our experiences at FSY London, where Jen and I served as Session Directors.

For us, FSY London served as a generous and inclusive space where we could prove our long-observed thesis - that our young people have a voracious appetite for truth and their faith in Jesus Christ will thrive in a radically inclusive environment that challenges and replaces entangled and outdated mindsets. With young adults leading youth, directing themselves and one another to Him, and trusting in everybody to advance, what we found (and what we have been able to build on since) feels important enough to share.

Creating Space for the Diversity of Circumstances

I feel like I can't be my whole self at church. I struggle to feel proud of who I am and where I've come from. Having to conform is really tough.

Malaika, 17

A friend, aged 16, recently said:

> We as a generation look for less judgement. We come to church to learn about Christ and to be accepted by our church community, no matter where we are on our journey. We don't come to tick every expectation box; we just want to be encouraged to be better, which will eventually help us to meet Church standards rather than to feel like we have to conform to a standard in order to be accepted. *There are many different ways to be good.*[04]

As leaders, teachers, and parents, we can help our young people to feel proud of who they are, where they have come from, and where they are on their *life-long* journey to Jesus Christ. Upfront arbitrary norms (defined perhaps as expectations that have no grounding in eternal doctrine or universal truth, and which aren't practised across all cultures and times) often become hurdles and hindrances—even if their parents or grandparents saw them as helps. Instead of confor-

04 Private Correspondence

mity, we can meet our young people where they are, and help them to feel loved, accepted, and supported. Their journey to Him starts with us inviting them to come as they are.

When Jen and I were called to serve as FSY Session Directors for London, there hadn't been an FSY session for three years; bringing the youth and young adults together in this way had become a casualty of the global pandemic. Those years were tough for so many.

As we considered our role, it felt important to create a bold and radically inclusive space for the rising generation to unite in their shared desire to come unto Christ. We felt a desire to plan content that would help connect them to Him as the source of all healing, recast a more inclusive lens over His core doctrines, and help them feel that the restored Church of Jesus Christ was their safe space.

The decision had already been made to invite all striving young adults to serve as counsellors, and not just returned missionaries. The twelve respective London stakes were focused on helping as many as possible to apply.

We surrounded the youth and young adults with a rich diversity of leadership, counsellors, and teachers—all of whom had incredible personal stories of faith and deep, personal connections to London. Perhaps most significantly, we decided to revise the session's local interpretation of the (at the time) culturally prioritised norms around dress and grooming standards (no long hair or piercings for boys, a strict single set of earrings for girls, no dyed hair, and a strictly upheld dress code). It had always been inappropriate to enforce such a narrowly defined set of expectations through ultimatum and threat of exclusion, and it certainly didn't fit with the inclusive space we sought to create.

Moreover, prior to signing their children's consent forms, many families and leaders contacted our team and shared their feelings that, for them, some of the expectations previously prioritised at church, and at FSY in particular, had been unhelpful. Post the global pandemic, these families wanted to more fully embrace a home-centred and Church-supported space for their children and were worried that if adjustments weren't made, exclusionary attitudes and behaviours would persist. Many sought assurances that we would turn the page and broaden the space to help their children come unto Jesus Christ.

In searching for our strategy, we remembered these words from Elder Jeffrey R. Holland of the Quorum of the Twelve Apostles. Where Elder Ballard had used the analogy of a boat, Elder Holland used the analogy of a choir. He said:

> I plead with each one of us to stay permanently and faithfully in the choir, where we will be able to savor forever that most precious anthem of all—"the song of redeeming love." Fortunately, the seats for this particular number are limitless. There is room for those who speak different languages, celebrate diverse cultures, and live in a host of locations. There is room for the single, for the married, for large families, and for the childless. There is room for those who once had questions regarding their faith and room for those who still do. There is room for those with differing sexual attractions. In short, there is a place for everyone who loves God and honors His commandments.[05]

We noticed that he didn't say "keeps perfectly His commandments." Rather he said "honors." He continued, with emphasis added:

"'*Come as you are*,' a loving Father says to each of us, but He adds, 'Don't plan to stay as you are.' We smile and remember that God is determined to make of us more than we thought we could be."[06]

Jen and I desired to flatten the path leading to the Saviour. Together with our team, we focused on a more inclusive invitation. Our ambition was that, at FSY, if the youth and young adults could feel accepted and loved unconditionally, they would more easily find the personal healing that comes only from the Saviour. We aimed to faithfully and carefully dismantle any distracting, local cultural norms and scrape off some of the barnacles. We made adjustments and replaced them with more spacious alternatives. We still had important rules to keep everybody safe and to establish boundaries. But those rules aligned to the sorts of rules you would find on school trips and summer camps.

---

05 Jeffrey R. Holland, *Songs Sung and Unsung*, General Conference (Salt Lake City: The Church of Jesus Christ of Latter-day Saints, April 2017), Gospel Library App.

06 Ibid

We wanted the youth and young adults to feel trusted and to exercise their agency in the commitments they would be invited to make. FSY is just a programme after all, and we were only its latest London custodians. As Elder Uchtdorf would later teach, "Jesus Christ *is* the strength of youth."[07]

Our strategy for FSY was formed approximately one year before the updated release of the *For the Strength of Youth – A Guide to Making Choices* pamphlet, which meant that our intentional changes weren't without feelings of inertia and trepidation. As word spread, where many felt excited, others felt nervous and even uncomfortable. Some felt the generous approach was inappropriate. Some parents wanted clarification that these changes were aligned to Salt Lake City and were concerned that FSY London would suffer from a lack of governance and would spin out of control. We privately questioned whether *control* was an appropriate word when seeking to inspire and invite young people to turn towards the Saviour and put their trust in Him.

We knew what we had felt, and we trusted our team of exceptional young adults who received their own witnesses and spiritual experiences of what we were unitedly trying to achieve. At FSY, we were determined to create the space that would detach the rising generation from outdated prejudices and reattach them to the Saviour, His doctrines, and deep feelings of validation, acceptance and belonging.

As a team, we launched our social media campaign, spearheaded by the hashtag of Elder Holland's invitation to #comeasyouare.

After a year of planning, the morning of FSY arrived. As the buses pulled in, Jen and I felt excited. As the youth filed out in their hundreds, a powerful spirit of inclusion filled our hearts. Everybody came ready to fill the space with their culture, their personalities, and their faith in Jesus Christ—no matter how fledgling or how mature. They had heard the spirit and tone of the invitation. They were their authentic selves. No hurdles had been placed in their way. Some of them had blue hair, some pink. There were earrings for boys and double-earrings for girls. One of the boys had a beautifully dyed leopard-print afro.

---

07 Dieter F. Uchtdorf, *Jesus Christ Is the Strength of Youth*, General Conference (Salt Lake City: The Church of Jesus Christ of Latter-day Saints, October 2022), Gospel Library App.

Some of them had nose piercings. Many of the boys had long hair and some wore beards. That day there were no off-ramps and no ultimatums.

As the week progressed, many of these incredible young people told us how they felt seen and heard. They said that because of this, they felt reassured that this was their space and their time to come unto Christ.

Thankfully, many that identify as LGBTQ+ came to FSY too. During the week some of them shared their faith in the Saviour. One of them said, "I have always felt that I would one day have to leave this Church that I love so much. This week I feel I want to stay and help create this kind of space for as many people as possible."

Come as You Are could be a tagline for membership in The Church of Jesus Christ of Latter-Day Saints. If not on the doors of our chapels, then, at the very least, in the hearts and minds of our members. *Come as You Are* is shorthand for *Come unto Christ as You Are.*

We read in the scriptures: remember the worth of souls is great in the sight of God.[08] He is no respecter of persons,[09] and has invited "all to come unto him and partake of his goodness; and he denies none that come unto him, black and white, bond and free, male and female; and he remembers the heathen; and all are alike unto God, both Jew and Gentile."[10]

Paul, in his epistle to the Philippians, wrote "in whatsoever state I am," (the Pauline equivalent of *Come as You Are*), "I can do all things through Christ which strengtheneth me."[11]

Jesus Christ said: "Come unto me, *all ye that labour and are heavy laden*, and I will give you rest. Take my yoke upon you, and learn of me; for I am meek and lowly in heart: and ye shall find rest unto your souls."[12]

Come as You Are is a validation of our starting point, a recognition of our circumstances, and a reassurance that He (and not others)

---

08 Doctrine and Covenants 18:10

09 Doctrine and Covenants 38:16

10 2 Nephi 26:33

11 Philippians 4:11,13

12 Matthew 11:28-29 emphasis added.

will give us rest as we turn, face, and then come unto Him. This rest could refer to the ultimate and eternal rest with Him and our heavenly parents, but it is also likely to refer to periods of rest in our lives when the difficult times come. It could be peace of mind, an inner feeling of calm, a healing of the body, heart, and mind, or a feeling of acceptance and belonging. It can be all those things and more. What a promise!

The rest Christ speaks of doesn't come from family or friends. It doesn't come from the Church, at least not directly. The full message of the invitation is for people to come as they are and, over time, feel restored by Him, in a way that is perfectly customised, perfectly stretching, and perfectly healing. It will take sacrifice, and yes, it requires that we act in faith. But trusting our young people, as opposed to telling them; helping them to find their own timetable, and not that of others, is hopefully an update we can all agree on.

Yet, despite this agreeable opener, too often we appear to create and prioritise a culture of conformity and standardisation, which is often exclusionary for far too many. Teaching the rising generation that there are arbitrary conditions and norms to live up to before they can feel safe, start, progress, or restart their personal faith in God, or before they can feel the influence of the Holy Ghost is at best unhelpful and at worst harmful.

Jesus prioritised lost coins,[13] lost sheep,[14] lost treasure,[15] and returning prodigals.[16] Moreover, He spent time with the marginalised, the blind,[17] the deaf and mute,[18] the lame,[19] the lepers,[20] the believing, and the doubting,[21] He never asked people to meet arbitrary standards before He extended His invitations, and it was ultimately their faith in Him that preceded His miracles. He also chastised and corrected any

13 Luke 15:8-10
14 Matthew 18:12-14
15 Matthew 13:44
16 Luke 15:11-32
17 Mark 8:22-25
18 Mark 7:31-37
19 John 5:2-9
20 Matthew 8:1-4
21 John 20:24-29

unjust in-groups creating cultures that excluded people. He was the ultimate space-creator as He invited them to follow Him.

The Gospel authors position struggling souls as the protagonists of Christ's stories, miracles, teachings, and general ministry. The Saviour heals people as they come as they are, and as they exercise their faith in Him. Our youth and young people do not have to earn His fondness through compliance to norms. God sent His Son[22] regardless of who accepts His invitation to repent and be restored.

When Jesus visits the Nephites, He summarises His doctrine by saying simply "ye must repent, and be baptised in my name, and become as a little child, or ye can in nowise inherit the kingdom of God."[23] Despite the simplicity and universality of His teachings, a lot more fine print has been added in the latter-days, including mindsets, expectations, attitudes, and behaviours—many of which have come to define our church culture. Although there are benefits to such a strong set of identifying markers, if not careful, they can become over emphasised and exclusionary to people trying their best.

Because of these mindsets, it is my observation that our faith tradition can at times inadvertently create and prioritise certain "in-groups." Before we realise it, our culture celebrates the in-groups and leaves the out-groups behind. Such in-groups might include returned missionaries, active members, temple recommend holders, priesthood holders, traditional two-parent families, married couples, full-tithe payers, multi-generational families, and even notoriety from a famous family name, amongst others. Perhaps in-groups form around the wealthy ones, the popular ones, the academic ones, or the musical ones.

In-groups can form when we thoughtlessly exclude sisters from council meetings, or when we don't give them a voice in decision-making. In-groups might form from calling the same people with the same backgrounds, skillsets, and experiences into leadership callings.

Our young people pick up on these subtle exclusionary behaviours. In many cases, their observations later become blocks to them learning to love their faith and feeling proud of it, especially in times when it feels fragile.

---

22 John 3:16

23 3 Nephi 11:38

Moreover, when we teach a sermon to our young people on a narrowly defined ideal (subtly promoting a particular in-group) we also teach the parallel sermon that those who cannot or have not yet achieved the same are somehow less than. This is why the living prophet teaches the doctrine of Christ and the principles of the gospel and not personal applications or interpretations. When we try to help by teaching our personal, narrow practicalities, we put many into an out-group. We create in-groups. These segregations create divisions and inadvertently exclude members instead of including them.

In the Book of Mormon, Alma led a mission to reclaim the apostate Zoramites, who were perverting the ways of the Lord. Although they denied the Christ, we can draw parallels between how they excluded others and how we need to keep our faith communities broad, inclusive, and welcoming, so that people can learn as they grow. The apostate Zoramites' dominant faith narrative was that they were the Lord's chosen people. Does that sound familiar?

> [T]hey did gather themselves together on one day of the week, which day they did call the day of the Lord . . . and [cried] . . . we believe that thou hast elected us to be thy holy children . . . thou hast elected us that we shall be saved . . . we thank thee that thou hast elected us . . . [E]very man did go forth and offer up these same prayers. . . . Now after the people had all offered up thanks after this manner, they returned to their homes, never speaking of their God again until they had assembled themselves together again to the holy stand.[24]

It's no wonder that Alma and his missionary team were "astonished."[25] Mormon, in his latter-day foresight, decided to include the account of the Rameumpton, rather than exclude it. Weighing the opportunity cost of his edit, the level of detail he included is significant. Even retaining its original curious name seems designed to catch our attention. It's as though he is saying to us in our day: "Look at this, right here. This matters!" Why? Perhaps because he wanted to warn against creating dominant mobs, or in-groups and out-groups within our religious communities. Among the apostate Zoramites, there was

---

24 Alma 31:12-23

25 Alma 31:12

no *Come as You Are*; only one set of attitudes and behaviours was permitted to prevail.

In the gospel of Matthew, Jesus taught a parable about a Sower who went forth to sow. As the writer recorded it, the seeds were sown without prejudice. Some fell by the wayside, some were devoured by the birds, some fell in stony places, and some in shallow soil where there wasn't enough depth for their roots to flourish. When the sun came out, these were scorched up and withered away. Others fell amongst thorns, and when the thorns sprung up, they were choked. Others, however, fell into good ground and brought forth fruit, some a hundredfold, some sixtyfold, some thirtyfold. Unusually, the author wrote that the Saviour gave a detailed explanation of the parable.

In this description, the seed was the 'word of the kingdom.' The different types of ground were different reactions to receiving the gospel message. Some received it and were led away. Some received it and fell away when persecution and tribulation came. Others were choked by what are described as the cares of the world and the deceitfulness of riches.[26]

It's easy to see how such a clear parable might lead us to create an in-group of 'fertile soil' members, and an out-group of those who don't yet want to (or can't or feel they can't) bring forth fruit. A certain tribalism can quickly take hold. Surely this is a justifiable mindset, we tell ourselves, as it comes from the mouth of the Saviour Himself! Creating a strong in-group identity of what it means to be faithful keeps our young people on track and keeps 'the world' out.

Heeding such warnings against temptation, pride, hard-heartedness, and apostasy is no doubt important. After all, where would we be without clear boundaries on what is right and what is wrong? Fences that keep the wrong influences out also double as boundaries and guardrails for those within the covenant. But when those fences keep young people from drawing near, or prevent them from feeling inspired and engaged, that is when the fences become a problem.

Could there be another layer to the parable for those "who hath ears to hear?"[27]

---

26 Matthew 13:3-23

27 Matthew 13:9

In Matthew 13, whilst God is undoubtedly the Sower, could an additional interpretation be that the seeds represent us—His children? In the language of the parable, in His perfect love and wisdom, God allows us to be planted in all manner of places, some in the fertile soil, others by the wayside, some of us in thorny places, and others in shallow soil. In the moments of our lives where we are able to bring forth fruit unto Him, for some it is a hundredfold, for others it is sixty-fold, and for others it is thirty-fold.

In order to settle the injustice of such a seemingly random sowing, and in order to overcome all of the inherent weakness and mortal conditions of the Fall of Adam and Eve, we are provided a Saviour to heal us and to bring us safely home. In the parable of the sower, could Jesus also be reminding us that there is endless differentiation in what our mortal experiences entail, by design? Could He be reassuring us that, despite our different places of planting, He labours to help us? But if this is the case, where is the resolution? How does He resolve the apparent randomness of our personal predicaments? To find that, we might borrow some light from the next parable.

Immediately after the parable of the sower, Jesus teaches the parable of the wheat and the tares.[28] This time, the kingdom of heaven is likened unto a man which sowed good seed in his field. As he slept, the enemy sowed tares amongst the wheat. Despite the disaster, the decision was made not to separate them until the harvest. At that time, the tares would be burned, and the wheat gathered in. Until then, the wheat would have to live with the tares.

When we sit atop our Rameumptons, trying to influence our young people, it can be easy to assume that the wheat represents the righteous and the tares represent the unrighteous – those who refuse to follow Christ or at least don't do it the way we all think they 'should.' The scriptures record that the disciples asked Jesus to explain this parable too. He appears to confirm the above view, suggesting the good seed are the 'children of the kingdom,' and the tares are the 'children of the wicked one.' Simple enough. Fortify the in-group and exclude the out-group until they conform. Jesus said so.

28 Matthew 13:24-30

However, if this is all we take from these parables, we are likely to misrepresent the true nature of our concerned and inclusive Heavenly Father and His Son whom He sent.

The realisation that there is divine design to the diversity of our circumstances helps to replace feelings of comparison with compassion and feelings of loss with love. Equally important to remembering that God plants His children in different places is to remember that He never plants any of them in places where they will fail or become overwhelmed by their personal tares.

All who come as they are unto Him, with their wheat and their tares, their wounds accrued throughout their mortal experiences, can and will be a success in the end. He alone will cast off their weakness—or their tares (personified as 'children of the wicked one'). Until He does so, the rest of us can be loving and supportive, doing our best to nurture the wheat.

All of us find ourselves in stony, arid, and thorny places by the wayside, because of our weakness. Jesus' invitations are personalised to our starting point and to our experiences. Why else would Jesus say to the certain young man who had kept all the commandments from his youth to "sell whatsoever thou hast and give to the poor, and thou shalt have treasure in heaven: and come, take up the cross, and follow me;"[29] whereas he said to the woman caught in the act of adultery to "go, and sin no more?"[30] The Saviour knows the circumstances of our planting, he knows our tares and personalises His healing. He invites us to come as we are and to act in faith. His "grace is sufficient."[31] There is so much more empathy and reassurance within these two parables when we apply an intentionally inclusive lens. It's that same lens we can passionately apply to our young people.

Come as You Are doesn't only extend to the new friends that the missionaries find and teach. That level of acceptance uses well-trained muscles. That level of tolerance can potentially be a righteous pride, another commendation, another merit badge, atop the Rameumpton.

---

29 Mark 10:20-21

30 John 8:11

31 Ether 12:27

No, the Christ-like empathy we are asked to learn extends to everybody on their terms and God's terms, not on our terms. Our empathy can extend to the young woman that is learning to find and express herself in her dress and appearance and the young man whose attitude and behaviour is masking his vulnerability and fear. Our empathy can extend to those young people who aren't yet ready to meet every standard historically emphasised by the faith tradition.

A loving and non-judgemental *Come as You Are* extended to the rising generation includes those exercising their agency and pushing or even rejecting boundaries. It extends to those who leave the Church and come back. It extends to those who leave the Church and don't come back. It extends to youth and young adults when they struggle to draw the same conclusions as their parents about their faith. It extends to young adults who go to university and find higher education incompatible with religious conviction. An attitude of *Come as You Are* keeps the door open and the lights on for everybody to one day turn towards the Lord and come unto Him.

It is so damaging to people's faith and spiritual security when these starting points and places of planting are ignored or overlooked. Consider how damaging it can be when we teach the realities of Christ's love and available mercy, but then, inadvertently, participate in and perpetuate a Rameumpton-like culture towards those who struggle. People struggle for all sorts of reasons. The Saviour doesn't ignore those reasons. Neither should we.

Inviting our young people to *Come as You Are* also includes those that have made mistakes and fallen from the covenant path. Although we may readily accept that all sins can be forgiven, we also have to accept that not all opportunities can be restored. But a merciful God can see beyond that too. In 4 Nephi, in describing the restoration of the Nephite infrastructure following the global destruction associated with the death of Christ, Mormon reminded us how a loving God moves us past our missed opportunities by giving us new ones. He says:

> And the Lord did prosper them exceedingly in the land; yea, insomuch that they did build cities again where there had been cities

> burned. Yea, even that great city Zarahemla did they cause to be built again. But there were many cities which had been sunk, and waters came up in the stead thereof; therefore these cities could not be renewed.[32]

When the choices of our young people are met with their consequences, often their former opportunities are no longer available. The unavailability of those opportunities can create anxiety. Consider the mission not served, the young adult divorcee, or those working through their repentance with their bishop.

When we allow our young people to truly come as they are, striving to do their best, exercising faith in Christ unto repentance, we avoid chaining them to their past mistakes. The Lord helps restore them by moving them on. To do so, He provides them with new opportunities. Helping the rising generation to come as they are means helping them progress onwards and not limiting them in what they can do at church. "In the kingdom of God, there are no second-class citizens."[33]

As teachers, leaders, and parents, we need to remember that the scriptures don't say 'Remember the worth of repentant souls is great in the sight of God,' or 'believing souls,' or 'high performing souls,' or 'obedient souls,' or 'tithe-paying souls are great in the sight of God.' Neither does it say 'modestly dressed souls,' or even 'clean-shaven souls,' or 'souls who don't identify as LGBTQ+ are great in the sight of God.' The revelation simply says 'souls.'[34]

Of course, we all need to repent. We need to make and keep covenant obligations. But that is between each of us and the Lord, and it is on the Lord's timetable, with the support of the bishop and the stake president if we want to participate in priesthood ordinances. Ultimately, there is a Judge. But, as our Creator, He alone owns the celestial definitions of desire, faith, humility, sincerity, sorrow, and repentance. Only He can look into our hearts and understand what resides there.

32 4 Nephi 1:7-9

33 David S Baxter, *Faith, Fortitude, Fulfillment: A Message to Single Parents*, General Conference (Salt Lake City: The Church of Jesus Christ of Latter-day Saints, April 2012), Gospel Library App.

34 Doctrine and Covenants 18:10

Before we came to earth, the value of their souls was worth the War in Heaven, worth the Fall of Adam and Eve, worth the infinite Atonement and Resurrection of Jesus Christ, and worth the Restoration of the gospel in the latter days. And all before they made a single choice or grew a single tare!

As we stood at the open doors of the coaches at FSY that first day, I felt emotional. I felt we were witnessing something truly special and felt the Lord's comforting approval that we were on His errand. That week, our team sought to create an environment where everybody (counsellors and youth: the rising generation) could grow in spiritual security, with a deep sense of inclusion and belonging, no matter their story, no matter their starting point, no matter their circumstances, no matter their missed opportunities, and no matter the level of commitments they were ready and prepared to make. Our role was to help flatten their on-ramp as they approached Him in faith, to create the space where they could feel that they belonged.

At FSY, we trusted the youth and young adults to choose Him and to find their own revelation on how to move forward, leaning into new stretching opportunities to find personal growth, and by making plans to receive their next ordinance. We trusted Him to nurture their faith and answer their prayers. We trusted them to learn how best to come unto Him through personal faith and personal repentance. We didn't love and trust them despite their circumstances. We loved them because of their circumstances. Their beautiful places of planting reminded us that the Saviour works with all of us, no matter our starting point and no matter our personal challenges. At the heart of it all was the invitation to start from where they were, no matter the past. By welcoming them and not judging or condemning them, through trust and not ultimatum, with them all safely gathered in, we set about connecting them to Him.

Chapter Summary

Many of our young people feel burdened by unreasonable expectations that don't validate their starting point or their personal circumstances.

We can help the rising generation understand that there are no arbitrary hurdles to come unto Christ and to exercise faith in Him.

Creating Space for Diverse Personal Connections

I like seeing my friends at church but if I'm really honest I'm not sure I can say I'm having a revelatory experience. When I do get close to having one, people only seem interested if the direction I receive matches up to what they thought I should have done in the first place.

Laura, 15

As our young people embark upon their journeys of faith, we can help them look inwards in ways that connect them directly to God. Through this connection, they can learn to create personal spiritual experiences. Without feeling connected to Him in this way, their local church experience can feel uncomfortable and even irrational. Understandably, people rarely hang around uncomfortable and irrational spaces. The rising generation are no different.

Importantly, connecting to God doesn't have to be earth-shattering. In my experience, these moments of connection are most often "small and simple."[35] At times, they can be just enough light and truth that a believing heart chooses to accept them as evidences that God lives, that He loves them, and that He is inviting them to move for-

35 Alma 37:6

ward. These experiences can come from the simplest of set-ups and in the most familiar of environments. Consider the following experience my friend gave me permission to share. It is included here because it shows one person's experience of what divine connection can feel like. His moment of feeling connected came through attending church.

> Early in our marriage, there was a time when I was really struggling in my faith. Despite having been a good missionary, it's fair to say that my church experience had become thin. Back then, we attended a ward of about 120, including maybe a dozen youth and a dozen Primary children. During that time, my wife briefly served as the ward Relief Society president.
>
> Every Sunday felt the same. Talks that repackaged general conference talks and what felt like an hour of being told how to live, how not to live, what to do and what not to do. It was so tough. In my mind, I would roll my eyes and shake my head at the stand-up routines that opened the meetings, or the insistence at reading out five minutes of announcements including the schedules of upcoming ward financial audits. Even the hymn selection would frustrate me. Even though I wasn't overly connected myself, I felt critical and cynical towards others' efforts.
>
> The quality of the testimony meetings and the lessons would bother me. Often our teacher just monologued for the full fifty-minute session. On most Sundays, to be completely honest, I held my phone up, pretending to follow the lesson or the scriptures. In reality, I would read the BBC Football analysis or the free national newspaper content. I might look at my social media accounts or send GIFs to my brother.
>
> Deep down I wanted to support my wife in her calling. She had always supported me in mine. She took it seriously and was good at it. The sisters loved her. Even so, I couldn't shake my frustrations and most Sunday mornings we would argue. Deep down, I was protesting that I had to go at all. One Sunday, I felt like I hit rock bottom.
>
> During the sacrament, I prayed. 'What is the point of all of this? How can all of this be You? I need more out of this experience. I need You to help me.' I didn't feel anything in that moment. I had forgotten it was the Primary presentation that day.
>
> Looking back, I don't remember all of the little messages and talks or even all of the songs the children sang. But I do remember them

singing a new song that I hadn't heard before and didn't learn when I was in Primary. After some thoughtfully written lines of verse, the song builds to, and repeats, an emphatic chorus:

"Gethsemane, Jesus Loves Me!

So he went willingly, to Gethsemane."[36]

I simply cannot put into words what came into my heart, during the repeating chorus. It was almost completely overwhelming. The words pierced me. I couldn't hide the tears. As I sat there in the pews of my very familiar chapel, I felt things that I can only describe as healing, mercy, and hope. I felt sorry for my weakness. But not because I was being corrected or rebuked. I just felt loved. Held in that moment, I remembered why I loved God and why I loved being a member of His Church. Something inside me reconnected. I felt like He knew me and loved me. I felt like He was reminding me how important I was to Him. I resolved to be better. I felt to try harder to repent of my cynicism. I didn't feel pressure to be perfect, but I knew I wanted to choose Him again as I began to feel made whole.

This experience is one of only a handful of spiritual witnesses I have received so far in my life. It came to me when I was sitting in my own chapel, in the very seats we always sit in. There was nothing particularly different about the build-up to the meetings that day, and it hasn't happened to me since. But that morning, I felt truly connected to Him. It has made all the difference. Since then, I have used the renewed spiritual momentum to embrace faith in Him, repent, and serve. Like Lego bricks, I have connected more to that experience, which in turn has connected me to Him.

These are the types of experiences that our youth and young adults need to be having; ones they can't have if they are concerned about the abuses they suffer as part of an 'out-group' instead of being focused inward. Creating local environments that help the rising generation make choices to receive revelatory experiences and use their agency will help them not only feel connected to Him but also to themselves. Being intentional in this way will help build spiritual resilience well beyond their young adulthood.

---

36 Melanie Hoffman, "Gethsemane," Salt Lake City: The Church of Jesus Christ of Latter-day Saints, 2018. Sacred Music App.

Perhaps with this in mind, President Nelson's first general conference address to the entire Church, as the new prophet, focused on personal revelation. In his talk entitled *Revelation for The Church, Revelation for Our Lives*, he reprioritised the powerful truth that God is our Father in Heaven and wants to help us. He said:

> One of the things the Spirit has repeatedly impressed upon my mind since my new calling as President of the Church is how willing the Lord is to reveal His mind and will. The privilege of receiving revelation is one of the greatest gifts of God to His children. . . .
>
> Imagine the miracle of it! Whatever our Church calling, we can pray to our Heavenly Father and receive guidance and direction, be warned about dangers and distractions, and be enabled to accomplish things we simply could not do on our own. If we will truly receive the Holy Ghost and learn to discern and understand His promptings, we will be guided in matters large and small.[37]

Balanced with these promises, he also shared a prophetic warning: "[I]n coming days, it will not be possible to survive spiritually without the guiding, directing, comforting, and constant influence of the Holy Ghost."[38]

Despite such clarity and encouragement, my observation is that we are prone locally to over programme our young people, instead of teaching them how to prioritise and establish personal divine connection. There is so much for them to learn, remember, and live up to in the Church, and so much content. Space and time to figure it all out can feel constrained.

President Nelson also taught:

> As we seek to be disciples of Jesus Christ, our efforts to *hear Him* need to be ever more intentional. It takes conscious and consistent effort to fill our daily lives with His words, His teachings, His truths. . . . It has

37 Russell M. Nelson, *Revelations for the Church, Revelations for Our Lives*, General Conference (Salt lake City: The Church of Jesus Christ of Latter-day Saints, April 2018), Gospel Library App.

38 Ibid

> never been more imperative to know how the Spirit speaks to you than right now.[39]

This generous charge creates space for our young people. It reminds them that God can and will guide them to personal answers to their personal questions. It is significant that the living prophet prioritised *personal* revelation in his first general address. *Personal,* because it is what they need to know, how to receive, recognise, and follow through on. But also *personal* because it will come in a way that they will understand. Now that doesn't mean that there won't be divine patterns to follow. But it does mean that when they need to find guidance, they can focus on making choices that connect them to Him instead of simply attending church and being a *good member*.

Helping our young people cultivate their own spiritual experiences and then being OK with what they feel they have received is key to creating space for them. If we override their experiences with local church expectations, they get mixed messages, and our young truth-seekers can be trampled in their best efforts.

When personal variation becomes a more culturally acceptable component of personal revelation and choice, we will know that we are truly empowering our young people. Their lives are different. Their starting points are different. Their circumstances are different. As such, their personal needs are also different. And yet we wonder why the space narrows when our advice to them becomes standardised or a template.

If we all adopted President Nelson's advice when seeking revelation and making choices, and we taught the rising generation to do the same, we would hold back from prescribed answers and instead teach them how to connect to Him. Beautifully, this is the tone and content of the newly published *For the Strength of Youth: A Guide to Making Choices*.

Perhaps then, we can acknowledge that we get ourselves into difficulties when the more dominant narrative is not to seek personal rev-

39 Russell M. Nelson, *Hear Him*, General Conference (Salt Lake City: The Church of Jesus Christ of Latter-day Saints, April 2020), Gospel Library App.

elation, but instead to make choices that comply with the established views of others. Of course the two are not mutually exclusive strategies, and the former is more difficult than the latter. But long-term success in helping young people find and retain faith is grounded in personal connection to God.

Here are a couple of practical examples:

A prodigious teenage rugby player has a career in elite sport unfolding in front of her. Committing to her talent will involve multiple weekly training sessions and occasional Sunday matches. Should she follow her dreams and find a way to make it all work?

For some, the reflex reaction would be to not entertain such an idea. A culture of online testimonials, Church magazine articles, Sunday talks, youth lessons, seminary, and firesides by inspirational athletes selected perhaps because they didn't compete on Sundays speak loudly. Interventions by family members, even late-night parental advice or arguments might also weigh heavily on her decision: "No need for revelation. This one is easy. Shut it down. We don't do that. Nor should you."

But remember the counsel of the living prophet. Shortcutting the opportunity to connect our teenage prodigy to Him in making her choice is a missed opportunity. By expressing her desires to Him in prayer, asking for His help, and seeking revelation from the Lord, she would likely find an enriching answer that would sustain her faith and strengthen her devotion to God.

Maybe she, herself, would conclude not to pursue the opportunities in front of her. That said, maybe she could become an elite, professional athlete, represent her country, and be a global ambassador for faith in Jesus Christ. Of course, there are many outcomes in between those two bookends which could help shape her life and bring her closer to God.

The point is that the role of those around her (the adult leaders, teachers, and parents) should be to help her prioritise the process of receiving personal revelation They should prioritise her personal discovery of how the Lord wants to bless her life and help her to make her own choice.

Another example where local cultural expectations can sometimes crowd out the reliance on personal revelation is how we support our young people in deciding to serve full-time missions.

Ever since the prophetic direction of President David O. McKay and later through President Spencer W. Kimball's 1974 charge for every worthy young man to serve a mission,[40] full time missionary service has been a community expectation and rite of passage amongst the rising generation. Elder Thomas S. Monson, then a member of the Quorum of the Twelve Apostles, said of the landmark talk in which the prophetic vision and charge were declared "[it] had profound and deep influence on all who heard it." He also said that "the impact of [President Kimball's] dynamics as a missionary-oriented person . . . have set in motion factors which have resulted in one of the greatest upsurges in missionary work that we have ever seen."[41]

President Kimball said:

> The question has been often asked, Is the mission program one of compulsion? And the answer, of course, is no. Everyone is given his free agency. The question is asked: Should every young man fill a mission? And the answer of the Church is yes, and the answer of the Lord is yes. Enlarging this answer we say: Certainly every male member of the Church <u>should</u> fill a mission, like he <u>should</u> pay his tithing, like he <u>should</u> attend his meetings, like he <u>should</u> keep his life clean and free from the ugliness of the world and plan a celestial marriage in the temple of the Lord[42] (emphasis in the original).

This prophetic prioritisation no doubt enabled the restored Church to scale rapidly and spread globally. Moreover, millions of lives have been blessed through the continuing global missionary programme of

40 Spencer W. Kimball, *Planning for a Full and Abundant Life*, General Conference (Salt Lake City: The Church of Jesus Christ of Latter-day Saints, April 1974), Gospel Library App.

41 "Status Report on Missionary Work: A Conversations with Elder Thomas S. Monson, Chairman of the Missionary Committee of the Council of the Twelve." *Ensign*, Salt Lake City, October 1977, Gospel Library App.

42 Spencer W. Kimball, *Planning for a Full and Abundant Life*, General Conference (Salt Lake City: The Church of Jesus Christ of Latter-day Saints, April 1974), Gospel Library App.

the Church, including my own. Encouraging the rising generation to have faith and to serve a mission is a good thing. Institutionally setting a standard is a good thing. There is no harm in inviting young people to stretch and sacrifice.

In April 2022, President Nelson renewed this prophetic charge and invitation. He said: "Today I reaffirm strongly that the Lord has asked every worthy, able young man to prepare for and serve a mission. For Latter-day Saint young men, missionary service is a priesthood responsibility."

Like President Kimball, his choice of language is both generous and notable. He said *asked* and not *commanded,* and he said *responsibility* and not *obligation.* Words matter. The Lord always works through invitation and persuasion. The prophet unflinchingly shares the Lord's invitation which gives us the space to choose and exercise our agency to rise to the opportunity. It's how we, as local leaders and parents then respond in the cultures and expectations we create that impacts our young people.

Said one:

> Nobody ever asked me if I wanted to serve a mission. Not one single person. All throughout my youth, the lessons, youth activities, and bishop interviews all focused on my mission. It was the only horizon I was ever given. I couldn't tell you how many sacrament talks I gave on the subject. I think I even wore a 'Future Missionary' badge in Primary. If I'm honest, I never really came to terms with serving, until I met my companion in my first area and I went to bed on my first night in the mission field. That night, I felt so alone. I knew it would break my mother's heart to come home early and I knew what happened to those who did so. I had seen it with my best friend's older brother. And so I served out the full two years. I enjoyed parts of it, but, once I came home, I realised that I had developed an awkward relationship with God and the Church. It was like I was living somebody else's life. I never felt connected to my choices, I guess. Eventually, I stopped attending. I wasn't angry or antagonistic, I just didn't feel it was for me. Before leaving, I felt lost for a while. I felt I had to find and build a new horizon in my life. I eventually went to university and found work, but it took me longer than it probably should have. I'm grate-

> ful for the values I learned at church and I enjoyed serving others on my mission, but I feel less anxious away from it all. I don't know what would have happened had the approach been different and the mission had felt more like my own choice. I guess, if I'm being balanced, I could have done more. But I was a kid. I think the invitations and expectations around me could have been more helpful.[43]

A culture of high expectations, when not connecting young people to Him, can present challenges to those who choose not to serve a mission, can't serve a mission, or go and then return home early from their mission. Although the Church has improved how proselyting missionaries teach through *Preach My Gospel*, and more recently moved to support in-field missionaries with more training, mentorship, and weekly video calls home, although there is an exciting and expanding global service missionary programme to broaden the opportunities for all, without helping our young people connect to God with their own spiritual experiences, long before they decide to serve, it is likely that many will continue to struggle.

In a renewed focus to connect them to Him and support personal revelation, we could do more to invite our young people to prepare for their missions by inviting them to seek their own call to serve through prayer and fasting and intentionally "studying it out in their mind."[44] Encouraging the rising generation to prayerfully consider "Does God want *me* to serve a mission?" would be an excellent accompanying narrative to the prophetic charge. But in order to be authentic, we also need to be OK with their considered and thoughtful decision resulting from such a revelatory quest.

With the Lord answering their prayers through His divine patterns, and with them acting in faith, with good advice and prophetic charges as supports, our young people could receive their call in their hearts long before the application was completed, the area assigned, and the call sent out. With this as the more dominant local narrative, desire to serve would come from a place of connection and not expectation.

---

43 Private Correspondence

44 Doctrine and Covenants 9:8

One can only speculate, but with such a revelatory experience underpinning their voluntary service, perhaps missionaries could serve with a greater sense of purpose and feel sustained by their experience long after they returned home. By being more intentional in their preparation, they will create more space for their discovery of how to receive and recognise answers to prayer, how to take leaps of faith when answers don't come, how to make choices based on righteous desires, and how to endure trials of faith.

If this is a stretch for leaders, teachers, and parents to accept, perhaps fearing that no young person will go along with such a generous local set-up accompanying the prophetic charge, we can rely on the fact that if the Lord requires every young man to serve, then He will support the sincere truth seeker in their vision quest and illuminate their minds to sign up.

We already use these faith muscles when teaching Moroni's promise[45] to those the missionaries are teaching. We know that inviting somebody to experiment with Moroni's promise is a sure way to connect them to the Source. Why not let that invitation be the same one we extend to the rising generation and their missionary service?

We have nothing to fear in trusting the rising generation. We do not need locally created fear or pressure to enforce expectations, even inadvertently. Identifying role models and removing silos between full-time missionaries, young adults, and youth would be helpful to support them in finding personal, intergroup, and intragroup inspiration. Over time, the best practices would emerge. But helping them to find clear answers to prayers and hear the voice of God in their lives would be a powerfully sustaining and space-creating experience.

Notably, in supporting the rising generation and their decisions to serve missions, we can draw confidence from observing the sister missionaries. The original 1974 charge, repeated in 2022, didn't apply to them. They can serve if they so choose. The distance these sisters have from expectations to serve gives them the space to thrive. When they choose to serve, it's because they feel called to the work. They feel a great desire to volunteer and include themselves, often because of

45 Moroni 10:3-5

special, personal experiences that have helped them feel connected to Him—exactly what we are looking for!

Of course, a more mature invitation would hopefully be met with reciprocal maturity. The invitation to seek personal revelation from God is less enabling if it is met with a hollow and empty "I prayed about it and the Lord said I don't have to." No; this refreshed narrative of trusting our young people to humble themselves, to study things out in their minds, to seek revelation, and to act in faith would require more from them and not less. For many it will be real work, involving soul-searching, fasting, prayer, and more time spent in temple environments. And that's really exciting!

Of course, when a young person rejects the invitation to serve and decides it isn't for them or comes home earlier than originally expected, we have an opportunity to respond with love and kindness, generosity and faith. Deep down, we all know that shunning, guilt tripping, or judging have no place in a united faith community. Although it might cause disappointment in the family, or in the ward, nothing should overshadow the love for and championing of the striving young man in question. His decision should not put him in an out-group. It shouldn't rob him of his dignity or his momentum. As he journeys to the Saviour, coming as he is, he still has opportunities to connect with God again and again.

It's difficult to imagine well-meaning, local leaders deliberately creating cultures that obstruct the path of our youth and young adults. But sometimes such messages are sent inadvertently or accidentally. Homecoming talks, homecoming open-houses, airport banners, and social media updates should become the welcome-wagon for all those that return and not just those who serve the full term. The absence of these heroic, trophy-experiences when a missionary comes home early can create a deafening silence.

Said one wise grandmother:

> You know, I never got it, until I saw my precious Grandson struggle. 10 years ago, I was in a different place. I guess I judged some of the young men who didn't serve. I think I may have even referred to them as 'failures to launch.' I feel so guilty about that today. I could have

> done so much more, back then. When my Grandson struggled with anxiety and came home from his mission early, as an insider to the full story, and all the things he experienced before and during his mission, I became his most loyal and fierce advocate. I wanted to fight for him and his faith in Christ like no other. At times, it broke my heart. I learned more from watching his courage and his struggle than from any other experience I have ever had.[46]

It is, of course, important not to rewrite the Prophet's teachings and suggest that serving a mission is not a priesthood responsibility. Sub-cultures of not heeding the prophet's counsel are not part of the Lord's plan or divine patterns. Missionary service is a priesthood responsibility. We all want our young men to fulfil their responsibilities. But we want them to do so in a way that helps them to thrive. When the rising generation become disconnected from their own inner voice, or from the promptings of the Spirit, in favour of the voices of others, faith becomes fragile.

The fact is that there are many who don't serve. When they don't, we want them to feel loved. We want to help them move forward on their faith journeys without being cast into an out-group which too often becomes a departure lounge for the eventual faith exit. The Lord rebuilds His people and their faith by giving them new opportunities—opportunities they can find and embrace as they connect to Him and seek their own personal revelation. Said a very dear friend:

> I didn't serve a mission. Back then, I wanted to study first and go to university. That's what my father did, and, at the time, he was my stake president. I planned to go later. When I was in my final year of study, I met my wife. We fell in love and decided to get married. Again, we were prayerful and did what we felt was right for us. We married in the temple and I'm now serving as a Bishop. I'm not saying for a moment that my way is (or was) the right way. I often think about the things I missed out on. I love the Lord; I strive to follow the prophet and I continue to strive to hear God's voice in my life. One thing I do know – today I would not be so strong in my faith, had the ward

46 Private Correspondence

> members and leaders not been so kind to me back then. Their love and respect helped me stay close to Christ.

The idea that we could trust the rising generation to come unto Him, seek (and find) direction for their lives through the Holy Ghost, and act in faith along their personal path isn't new. One of the purposes of the Restoration as described by the Lord Himself was to increase faith in the earth through enabling individualised personal revelation. In the first section of the Doctrine and Covenants, a section that was added later to help frame the revelations, we read:

> Wherefore, I the Lord, knowing the calamity which should come upon the inhabitants of the earth, called upon my servant Joseph Smith, Jun., and spake unto him from heaven, and gave him commandments; . . . that every man might speak in the name of God the Lord, even the Savior of the world; That faith might also increase in the earth.[47]

In the Old Testament, there is a clearer example of the benefit of trusting our young people and why the Lord arranged it so that we give the gift of the Holy Ghost to every newly baptised member of His church.

> And Moses went out . . . and the Lord came down in a cloud, and spake unto him . . . But there remained two of the men in the camp, the name of the one was Eldad, and the name of the other Medad: and the spirit rested upon them; and they were of them that were written, but went not out unto the tabernacle: and they prophesied in the camp. And there ran a young man, and told Moses, and said, Eldad and Medad do prophesy in the camp. And Joshua the son of Nun, the servant of Moses, one of his young men, answered and said, My lord Moses, forbid them. And Moses said unto him, Enviest thou for my sake? would God that all the Lord's people were prophets, and that the Lord would put his spirit upon them.[48]

Clearly this is "prophets" with a lower case 'p.' Only one man is sustained and authorised to hold and exercise all priesthood keys upon

---

47 Doctrine and Covenants 1:17, 20-21

48 Numbers 11:24-29

the earth. However, being a prophet in our own lives is another way of saying that we are authorised to seek and find personal revelation as we build our faith in Jesus Christ. Moses wished that all his people were prophets—and surely he included the rising generation in his desire. If Moses trusted the young people to prophesy and wished they would all do it more, perhaps there is a pattern there for us to follow.

We don't know exactly what the young men in the camp prophesied about, we just know that it pleased Moses and he wanted more people to do the same. We also know that it made others feel uncomfortable. As such, an important qualification would be to teach our young people that such closeness to the Holy Ghost and the resulting gift of prophecy would be for their personal lives and spheres of responsibility. It would not extend to 'receiving revelation' on behalf of others, in a way that over-writes their personal agency or choices.

We can trust our young people to qualify for, find, and follow revelation when connected to Christ as the Source of all revelation. Yes, of course they need guides, mentors, and role models reminding them of doctrine and teaching them the principles that govern it. But those role models should not print onto them their own expectations based on what worked for them. No. Their role models, mentors, and guides can instead connect them to God.

When the rising generation make what turn out to be poor decisions, either because they struggle to receive answers to their prayers, become weary and fatigued or even because they choose to rebel, they don't need our judgement; they need hope, respect, and repentance, which is also between them and God. Whilst Bishops and Stake Presidents hold the keys to help them unlock access to covenants and ordinances, the rest of us can love, empathise, and support.

But at times it seems that the straight and narrow path seems to have become straighter and narrower for our young people. Why is that? Perhaps part of the answer is that too often we inadvertently connect people to the connectors and not to the Source: Jesus Christ.

Consider the difference between the Source and a third party pointing us to the Source in the following example:

The Book of Mormon records that the risen Lord does many things during His first visit to the Nephite people. Once the Father presents Him as the Only Begotten, Jesus Christ introduces Himself and confirms that His condescension, including Atoning Sacrifice and Resurrection, are complete. Significantly, He then invites the multitude to go forth and feel the prints of the nails in his hands and in his feet and the wound print in his side. This is not a sermon from a tower, tablets from the mountain-top, or shouted from the city wall. This is a personal witness, one by one, one to one. He connects every one of them to Him, the Source. It is given to each of them to know that He is Christ resurrected. They know with certainty that He is the God of Israel, the promised Messiah who had been slain for the sins of the world. Mormon doesn't include how long this experience took, but forging these connections is the first thing Jesus does. It is His first priority. Each member of the multitude has a personalised experience with Jesus Christ. Significantly, the profound nature of the connection ushers in a period of two hundred years of peace. "[T]here was no contention in the land, because of the love of God which did dwell in the hearts of the people."[49]

Some four hundred years earlier, King Benjamin's service, leadership, and example also have a marked effect on his people. He also gathers his people to the temple. He also teaches the divinity of "Jesus Christ, the Son of God, the Father of heaven and earth."[50] At the end of his sermon, he also sees great success. When calling out to his people for their response, they cry with one voice:

> Yea we believe all the words which thou hast spoken unto us; and also, we know of their surety and truth, because of the Spirit of the Lord Omnipotent, which has wrought a mighty change in us, or in our hearts, that we have no more disposition to do evil, but to do good continually.[51]

King Benjamin successfully connects his people to the Source – at least for a season. Later in the Book of Mosiah, Mormon reminds us that the connection doesn't last:

---

49 4 Nephi 1:15

50 Mosiah 3:8

51 Mosiah 5:2

> Now it came to pass that there were many of the rising generation that could not understand the words of King Benjamin, being little children at the time he spake unto his people; and they did not believe the tradition of their fathers.[52]

Both Christ Himself and King Benjamin prioritise connecting their people to Jesus Christ and His power to rescue, heal, and save. However, whereas the direct connection lasts four generations, the indirect connection lasts barely thirty years. The profound nature of a direct, personal connection to God affects the ancient American society with righteousness for two hundred years.[53] King Benjamin, good as he is, spiritual as he is, isn't able to create a fraction of the connection that Christ creates. Without their own personal connection, akin to what their parents have felt, King Benjamin's rising generation doesn't find their way forward in their faith.

Be it the will of parents, teachers, leaders, peers, a sense of duty, habit, routine, or even prophets, connecting our young people to things other than Christ will not have the power to build and sustain faith in God over time.

However, sometimes the local experience can seek a more narrow, one-size-fits-all approach.

The two hundred years since the establishment of The Church of Jesus Christ of Latter-day Saints has created a lot of material, especially when the learning model keeps it ever present and on a regular cycle. We rarely retire content. We just keep adding. All of us sit through stake and ward conferences, weekly sacrament meetings, Sunday lessons, Seminary, and Institute lessons that quote a long history of Church materials and manuals. If what our young people need is living water, our oral traditions and recycled materials pose the risk of turning them into the ancient Mariner, who when thirstily confronted by his oceanic landscape cried "water, water, every where, Nor any drop to drink!"[54]

---

52 Mosiah 26:1

53 4 Nephi 1:24

54 Samuel Taylor Coleridge, "The Rime of the Ancient Mariner," *Lyrical Ballads: 1798 and 1802 (Oxford World's Classics)*. Oxford University Press, Oxford, UK, 2013. 5.

Moreover, if we are not careful, a high-performance culture can emerge around those who can remember more of the content than others or who can present it best in front of a congregation. In-groups create out-groups, and out-groups get excluded.

Perhaps it is not only the volume of repeated content that has created templates but the delivery method as well. Church can be a passive experience of one-way sacrament sermons and classroom-based presentations. Some teachers are no doubt more effective than others in creating learning environments, but the default of sit-and-listen-whilst-we-tell-you-things can take a toll. In an effort to try and tidy it up, *Come, Follow Me* is far less prescriptive and far more engaging with its open question style—educating the heart as well as the mind. *Come, Follow Me* represents a concerted effort to support members in their study routines. There is strength in a united community. For those who find it helpful, today's content is certainly more enabling of personal connection than we have seen before.

But it's not easy. The repetition can be difficult. Depending on the local approach, young people can find themselves encouraged to study personal *Come, Follow Me*, family *Come, Follow Me*, attend bi-monthly Sunday School lessons from *Come, Follow Me*, and attend daily seminary lessons on *Come, Follow Me*. The overlap can be intense. In case that wasn't enough, this content has been added to by a pandemic-created, self-appointed, and unofficial community of YouTube teachers and podcasters. Don't misunderstand me, I love podcasts. It's not the variety of content that causes the challenge. The challenge comes, at times, from local encouragement to consume all of it, especially when it comes across as a quasi-commandment or becomes associated with being a *good member*.

We also have to remember that all of this content is administered by imperfect, well-meaning, most-often-untrained, local, volunteer members; like us! This can complicate our ability to create connecting experiences akin to the Nephite multitude connecting to Him, or my friend's experience in his local Primary presentation.

As leaders, teachers, and parents, we can do more to reassure and unburden the rising generation. We can help them curate their own materials and, through prayer and study, connect directly to Jesus

Christ by having revelatory experiences through the Holy Ghost. Everything else is ultimately insufficient to support our young people longer term. They need living water. They need connection. Thinking creatively around how to do this, harmonising seminary, Sundays, and personal study will no doubt support their seeking.

There is, of course, nobody to blame for the challenges of organised religion and centralised curriculum committees. It is entirely understandable that a central model creates and curates content for a global membership. Empathetically, President Dieter F. Uchtdorf taught in 2015:

> Sometimes we take the beautiful lily of God's truth and gild it with layer upon layer of man-made good ideas, programs, and expectations. Each one, by itself, might be helpful and appropriate for a certain time and circumstance, but when they are laid on top of each other, they can create a mountain of sediment that becomes so thick and heavy that we risk losing sight of that precious flower we once loved so dearly. Therefore, as leaders we must strictly protect the Church and the gospel in its purity and plainness and avoid putting unnecessary burdens on our members.[55]

Perhaps the experience of participating in the Church and our learning culture can feel sedimentary at times. Feeling like that would make us normal. Trying to drink the ocean will bloat any stomach. When our young people feel overwhelmed, we can role model how we personally connect to the Source. By so doing, we will help our young people forge their own connections through personal prayer, personal study (of their own curated materials), personal reflection, patience, and personal revelation. We need to help them understand that hearing, understanding, and following Him is a lifetime pursuit.

At FSY, our young adult counsellors prepared their own personalised devotionals, having studied, prayed, and fasted for direction. Through personal connection and personal faith, they in turn invit-

---

55 Dieter F. Uchtdorf, *It Works Wonderfully!*, General Conference (Salt Lake City: The Church of Jesus Christ of Latter-day Saints, October 2015), Gospel Library App.

ed the youth to take similar steps to forge their own connections. Said one of our youth:

> The morning devotionals were my favourite part of FSY. Even though it was really early, I felt the Spirit so strongly. I felt like God was with me. I felt the messages were handpicked just for me. I'd never really understood how to apply the scriptures to my life but during those devotionals, shared by my incredible counsellor, I felt like I tapped into something completely different. I was able to say with confidence that I was feeling the Spirit.[56]

The rising generation of young adults and youth can do this if we will only let them. Calling our young adults to opportunities to work closely with the youth, in a way that helps create and prioritise personal divine connection with Christ will bring great rewards. In many cases, we will need to challenge our learning environments to ensure the focus is on helping establish these diverse personal connections.

Chapter Summary

Many of our young people feel judged for their choices, as if their voice matters less than the voices and opinions of others. This often leaves them feeling like they really only have two choices: conform or exit.

We can celebrate differences in how our young people practise their faith and hear His voice because we can trust that God has a different path for each of His children.

---

56 Personal Correspondence

Creating Space for Uncertainty

People are so certain about everything at church. I don't feel like I know much at all and, deep down, that really bothers me. Because I can't say I know for sure, I tend to say nothing at all.

Isaac, 16

PICTURE A FAST AND TESTIMONY MEETING. HOW MANY TIMES IS THE following, or a variation of the same, heard over the pulpit?

"I know the Church is true and that it is the only true church upon the earth. I know that God lives and I know that Jesus is the Christ. I know that the Book of Mormon is the word of God. I know that Joseph Smith was a prophet of God . . ."

Over the years, I have attended many meetings and trainings designed to remind people how to bear a testimony. Whether it was a fifth Sunday lesson, or Ward Council, or other training, I have listened to people weigh the declarations of faith by others that did not fit this template. I have also heard much discussion about where various fixes to those declarations should be applied. In each case, the motive was to seek to elevate the level of inspiration in the testimony meetings by helping members choosing to share their faith in a more Christ-centred way and to avoid random, extemporaneous commentary that distracted from people's Sabbath worship.

All of this is OK, but we misstep when we perpetuate a language and culture of certainty as the only means to communicate something as personal and, at times, fragile as faith. The priority seems to be for people to *bear* their testimony as opposed to *bare* their testimony. Whilst the former might well be inspiring and instructive, the latter brings more authenticity and more vulnerability. In my experience, the testimony meetings that achieve such vulnerability are by far more inspiring. I leave those meetings feeling not only more connected to my ward family but also to my own weakness and therefore my own dependence on Christ.

However, many of the testimony meetings I experience don't commonly feature this level of authenticity or vulnerability. Not only does the language of "I know" narrow the space, but it encourages people to double-down on the absolutisms. Saying things like: "I know without a shadow of a doubt," or "I know with every fibre of my being," or "I bear my witness" may be strong linguistically, but they do not strengthen those struggling with feeble faith. In many cases, these lines are copied from senior apostles and prophets who have used them in the past in their capacity as special witnesses.

Interestingly, the first recorded general conference reference to 'every fibre of my being' in bearing testimony of the gospel was Elder John Henry Smith in 1885 as a member of the Quorum of the Twelve Apostles serving under John Taylor as President (the same John Taylor who survived Carthage Jail).[57] The last time the phrase was used at general conference was by Elder Legrand Richards in 1958 holding the same office, although under the presidency of David O. McKay. Similarly, the first time "shadow of a doubt," was used was in 1855.[58] It was used by Elder Jedediah M. Grant of the Quorum of the Twelve.

Obviously, the opportunity to testify when invited, either at the end of a talk, lesson, or during fast and testimony meeting, under the direction of the bishop, belongs to anybody who wants to declare their faith in Jesus Christ. Moreover, they have the right to declare their faith in any way they so choose. The last thing I want to do is create a reverse in-group, 'othering' those who feel it is important for them to declare their personal certainties in what they feel is their safe space.

---

57 lds-general-conference.org. Search: "Every fibre of my being." Search result 17. November 29th, 2023.

58 lds-general-conference.org. Search: "Shadow of a doubt." Search result 48. November 29th, 2023.

We want to break down walls, not build them up again. Creating space for everybody really does mean everybody. Some people react well to fervent declarations of faith and zeal. It can inspire people and give tacit permission for others to believe the same. Statements of truth also invite the influence of the Holy Ghost whose responsibility it is to testify of truth.[59]

That said, a culture of certainty can narrow the space for those who don't yet feel the same conviction or enthusiasm. Those who are trying to figure it all out as they go need as much space for their uncertainty as those who have space for their certainty. This is especially true for our young people.

We can ask ourselves: what else grows in a culture of certainty? When are we encouraging all to choose to come unto Christ? What does this approach do to people when their tares grow up or they find themselves sown in difficult times and places? How does it make people feel when they don't feel they 'know' anymore? What does it do to people who struggle as their faith matures, or are challenged by what they once felt they knew? What does it do to our young people who are trying to figure out if faith in Christ is something they can trust or something they want to participate in? If absolute certainty is the only available language of expression, the resulting narrowness and inflexibility can make faith brittle and liable to breaking. Pushing people into an 'all-in' or 'all-out' dilemma is dangerous for a generation that wants authenticity and vulnerability. Such environments are unhealthy for our young people and are at odds with the Lord's divine pattern of "line upon line."[60]

Within this culture of certainty, I have observed that some of those who walked away from their faith talk about a 'shelf-break moment.' Usually with hindsight, they believe they can pin-point when they first began to entertain the idea that their certainties were no longer guaranteed. Sometimes, that moment is when they first felt that their values were no longer reflected in their experience in, or with, the Church. The metaphor is of a shelf bearing a load it was never designed to bear. With inappropriately applied weight, at first, the shelf

59 John 15:26; Moroni 10:5; John 14:16-17

60 Isaiah 28:10

bows in the middle; then, as more weight is applied; it cracks. Finally, the shelf breaks and all of the once cherished items (books, ornaments, etc.) end up lying in a damaged or broken heap on the floor.

Shelf-breaks are traumatic experiences for those impacted. Having spent time in these spaces with people, they are sacred places and often don't have immediate resolutions.

For some, heavier loads can include newly discovered information from Church history, personal discomfort with Church policies (past and present), unrealistic local expectations, impatience, or fatigue with the quantity of volunteer opportunities and the lack of varied volunteers, or the behaviours of people they are required to sustain as leaders called by God.

Many of our young people deal with broken faith shelves. Many are currently living with cracked faith shelves—their loads and burdens have been and are too heavy.

However, the great thing about shelves is that they can be intentionally moved, strengthened, and replaced with other furniture—including bookcases and other cabinetry. The furniture of faith has many models and designs, allowing us to dress our spaces as we need.

Such moments of heavier loads and bowing shelves always need intentional furniture redesign. Staying connected to Him is important, but so too is cultivating a broader vocabulary which can often lead to a broader mindset.

If 'I know' is the only language people have to describe their experiences, it's no wonder that shelves can and do break. If the only options we give ourselves are to keep loading the shelf or to let it all drop to the floor, no wonder so many can and do struggle.

I always feel sad when young people relinquish their entire faith in God because of frustrations at church. People need to feel safe, and they will have their own reasons for stepping back. But when the shelf starts to creak, it isn't the time to quit on faith; it's the time to broaden it, strengthen it, and transition it. Such moments are great opportunities to connect to God and intentionally strengthen or replace old furniture which no longer serves their needs. Moving through and beyond the challenge because of the challenge is when personal growth takes place. We can all personally grow through more connected religious experiences.

Teaching a more spacious language of faith to the rising generation, helping their faith to mature and transition beyond the simplicity of their valuable Primary lessons would help so many. One place to start is to grow comfortable saying "I don't know."

Within our tradition, we are comfortable with the words "I know." They are said much more often than "I don't know." Across the history of recorded General Conferences, the phrase "I know," has been said 12,242 times at the time of writing.[61] By comparison, "I do not know," has been said only 1,929 times (6.3 times less).[62] Evidently, these phrases aren't all linked to faith or the search for faith, but it is interesting to see the contrast. Getting more comfortable with "I don't know," and seeing it as the beginning of faith and not the end of it, is important.

In the Book of Mormon, Alma teaches that the construction of faith starts in a state of not knowing and leads us to a place of believing and only then onto a place of knowing. Sometimes we unsympathetically forget the beginning of that journey, ignoring the fact that the start of Lehi's dream saw him battle a dark and dreary wilderness.[63]

Returning to the Zoramites, in Alma 32 we find them evicted from their synagogues because of their poverty. Alma, in response, teaches them about humility and faith. Struggling in their faith, the ejected Zoramites are not dissimilar from our rising generation. To tend to their needs, Alma teaches them the process of a spiritual experience. His choice of language is notable. He says:

"Faith is not to have a perfect knowledge of things . . . God is merciful unto all who believe on his name . . . Ye cannot know of their surety at first, unto perfection."[64]

---

61 lds-general-conference.org. Search: "I know." Search result 1. November 29th, 2023.

62 lds-general-conference.org. Search: "I do not know." Search result 1. November 29th, 2023.

63 1 Nephi 8:4, 7

64 Alma 32:21-22, 26

Alma uses small, light, and inviting vocabulary. He moves his audience away from the idea of certainty and instead starts them off with the vocabulary of desire. And yet, if people were to stand up in fast and testimony meeting today and say "I don't know if any of this is true; I have some serious doubts. But I'm here. I want to learn, and I want to grow my faith in God," feelings of discomfort would likely grip the meeting. But where we might feel uncomfortable, Alma would likely rejoice. He continues:

> [E]xperiment upon my words, and exercise a particle of faith, yea, even if ye can no more than desire to believe, let this desire work in you, even until ye believe in a manner that ye can give place for a portion of my words.[65]

For Alma, the more appropriate starting point for faith construction is desire and reassuringly creating space for that desire. Said one of our older young men at FSY:

> I've never been all that churchy. But more recently I felt it was important to give my testimony another go. My bishop has been really helpful. He hasn't put pressure on me. We've spent a lot of our time talking about what it means to come unto Christ and how He is first and foremost our rescuer and healer. I've found that to be a great place to start to learn about the desire to believe. I'm still not sure what I want to do, but I feel good talking about faith as a journey.[66]

The Zoromites Alma and Amulek teach don't have space for their faith. So, in turn, Alma and Amulek counsel them to make their own space in their hearts. As they begin to connect with the Source, now unencumbered by the traditions of their community, he explains what a spiritual experience with God *feels* like. But he still moves slowly.

Said one of our young women:

> I like that my faith is a journey and not an immediate destination, and I like that it's expected that there will be highs and lows. I feel like I know enough to want to learn more. I find it much more motivating

65 Alma 32:27

66 Personal Correspondence

> to consider myself as somebody who is growing faith in Jesus Christ. I really admire those who say that they *know*. I'd like to grow to that place too one day, but I've learned from my parents that it's OK if this takes time.[67]

Alma leads the Zoramites through an upward spiralling, faith journey from desire to knowledge. He knows that faith starts with desire and not certainty. He recognises that in time desire grows into certainty through experience.

In our day, we might say to the rising generation: "Don't fret if you don't feel you know and you hear others declaring their confidence and conviction. That is totally normal. Why don't you start with choosing to believe? Why don't you follow the words of Christ, act in faith, and do some things that will draw you nearer to God? As you do that, you'll start to feel more confident. Worry less about what others think or tell you or what you see and hear them do. You can do this. In time, with more experiences, as both Moroni and Alma taught, 'you may know the truth of all things.'"[68]

At FSY, we observed how such generous learning environments create space for the rising generation to come unto Christ. During the week, the schedule includes an evening of testimony sharing. In order to help all feel comfortable, the testimony meetings are split into smaller groups of 50-60 participants and organised by age.

For some, being encouraged to share their faith in such a way is an exciting experience that can form key milestones along their faith journey. As they hear themselves share their faith, it can in turn create more faith. That said, for others, sharing their faith can feel uncomfortable and overwhelming. Public speaking is hard enough. The thought of sharing something so personal can be a real stretch; especially if they feel that it may be poorly framed in their mind, in front of their peers, in language that feels inauthentic because they don't yet feel that they own it.

Before these testimony meetings began, we taught a devotional on how to share a testimony and create more space for ourselves and oth-

---

67 Personal Correspondence

68 Moroni 10:5

ers. Instead of repeating the familiar "keep it short, keep it simple, and keep it Christ-centred," we talked about how being more intentional in our vocabulary allows us to own what we are saying by creating vulnerable and authentic connection with ourselves and others.

We taught the virtues of embracing 'I don't know,' and that such a phrase doesn't need to be feared. 'I don't know,' can create more space for wondering and searching, pondering and praying. Not knowing is a forerunner to asking questions, and questions eventually lead to answers.

If everything, from the very beginnings of learning, is couched in a language of certainty – where is the need to experiment (using Alma's word)? His word for searching and asking was 'nurturing.' That's how faith grows.

As leaders, teachers, and parents we can encourage the rising generation to experiment, nurture their faith, and find peace in the calm language of uncertainty. Where some might find discomfort and risk in "I don't know," others can find their beginnings, or their resting place with more faith, more mystery and more devotion to God.

Not knowing something isn't a vice. Consider these two examples: one from Nephi and one from President Gordon B. Hinckley. Said Nephi: "I know that God loveth His children; nevertheless, I do not know the meaning of all things."[69] And President Hinckley said: "I wish to give you my testimony of the basic truths of this work. I confess that I do not know everything, but of some things I am certain."[70]

Accepting that we don't know something creates space for hope and trust in God. From there we can act in faith. If a language of certainty is the only means we provide for the rising generation to express themselves, saying things that they don't yet own may cause them to feel that they are using somebody else's words. In time, they may start to feel that it is somebody else's space, somebody else's church, and somebody else's faith.

---

69 1 Nephi 11:17

70 Gordon B. Hinckley, *The Things of Which I Know*, General Conference (Salt Lake City: The Church of Jesus Christ of Latter-day Saints, April 2007), Gospel Library App.

Perhaps by broadening our vocabulary and relying on alternative language to "I know" in the near term, we can help them to feel more intentional and authentic.

What about the following as space-creating openers to testimony sharing?

I hope . . .
I believe . . .
I pray . . .
I search . . .
I ponder . . .
I wonder . . .

At FSY, the rising generation were grateful for the content.

That evening, across the testimony meetings, one at a time the youth and young adults stood to share their faith. It was as though their hearts had been set free. Beautifully sincere, declarations of faith filled the breakout rooms for the next two hours. One by one they stood to share where they felt they were on their faith journeys to Jesus Christ.

Some testimonies were bold and decisive, whilst others were meek and timid. Some were longer, some shorter. Some were very short. Across the groups, we had some powerful 'I knows,' balanced with countless 'I believes,' 'I hopes,' and 'I prays,' and even some 'I don't knows,' and 'I wants.' One stood and cried as she tenderly said: "I'd like to share my faith. I hope all of these things are true. I hope there is a God. I hope that He loves me. I hope that when I meet Him, He will give me a hug even though I am gay." Many were visibly moved by not only her courage but also by how she was authentically sharing her desires and fledgling faith in her Saviour. She was later warmly embraced by her friends and young adult counsellors as they expressed their deep love for her.

The object here is not to place taboos on how or what people can or should say. But making space for everybody is what Jesus would do. There is no more virtue in an 'I believe' than there is in an 'I know.' The last thing we need is to roll our eyes at the 'I knows.' That misses the point and replaces one exclusionary narrative with another. Alma makes it clear that faith does eventually grow into perfect knowledge and certainty. In 1820, Joseph Smith himself summarised his own extraordinary experience in the grove of trees as "I knew it and I knew that God knew it."[71] So let's not fall into the rather obvious trap!

The Sunday after FSY, the stake presidents were invited to create space for the youth to bear their testimonies in their home wards. Throughout the morning, whilst we sat in our home ward reflecting on our own faith in Jesus Christ, our phones were exploding with messages in our leadership chat. Our team was excited to share with one another what they were seeing and feeling. Youth of all ages were standing at the pulpits, claiming them as their own safe spaces. But this time it was different. This time they were using a different language. This time they were baring their faith and not just bearing their testimonies; lots of "I believes," lots of "I hopes," lots of "I feels," and a lot of "I knows."

Interestingly, from one ward, a report was shared that some of the older members had become uncomfortable with what was happening. In this ward, the faith declarations of a young woman choosing the "I don't know yet" vocabulary triggered a long line of more senior testifiers rising to defend the faith, as though their own sacred space had become unsafe. In turn they stood to say things like "I need the youth to know that I *know* – with zeal and emphasis added – that the Church is true." Those who were there felt the experience had trampled something pure that had begun to take hold in the meeting of that morning.

At FSY, we shared our own faith often. It felt important to model the broader options available. We said things like:

"We have faith in Jesus Christ and in our Heavenly Father's plan. We believe in Them and strive to follow Them. We know that when we draw near to Them through prayer and reading the scriptures, we feel hope, clarity, and peace. We have had many spiritual experiences and a few undeniable witnesses that clearly signal to us that faith is a blessing. Sometimes living up to it is difficult, but we are so grateful for repentance and the opportunity to reset and go again."

It was a long way away from "I know the Church is true."

---

71 Joseph Smith—History 1:25

The language we use matters. Intentionally owning what we say and expressing it authentically validates our starting point and our circumstances. The rising generation know this better than anybody. Encouraging them to be their authentic selves and speak the truths they know, those they believe, and those they are still learning to love, is a path to a more sustainable faith in their Saviour.

Chapter Summary

Authenticity and vulnerability are important values held in common by the rising generation. Yet many of them feel these qualities are too often missing from their church experience.

By creating more space for uncertainty, particularly in how we describe matters of faith, we can more quickly build an inviting and inclusive space for all.

Creating Space for the Diversity of Families

How can my family possibly fit into God's plan?

Shanequa, 19

Despite our best efforts to make more inclusive changes within our local communities, some of our young people might say: "Yes, a culture of coming as I am that prioritises my personal connection to God above everything else, together with a more inclusive vocabulary, will indeed create a more refreshing and authentic space. And I am excited by that. Unfortunately, that doesn't address the elephant in the room. What about the exclusionary things we are taught to believe? That's the source of my pain. That's what causes the rifts in my family. My dad doesn't believe, and my siblings have decided that our faith isn't for them. It's the conflict of knowing the consequences of their choices that hurts me the most. Why would I want to inherit an eternity that is different to where my family is headed?"

That would be an understandable response. And here there are opportunities to – perhaps more delicately – scrape some of the barnacles off of our anchored traditions.

Although the doctrines of Christ as taught by Him are pure and can be relied upon, challenges in tone and narrative come from many places. History, mindsets, sedimentary layers of past teachings, past emphasis, and what we might call the messy middle of volunteerism, all play their part in adding barnacles to our faith traditions.

Because our learning culture very rarely includes any official ground-clearing, rarely deletes or confines outdated paradigms to their time (at least publicly), and because of our cultural conviction around following the prophet (and inertia to anything he doesn't explicitly teach), it can be difficult to turn the page. Scraping the barnacles off the boat can become a laboured exercise and sometimes it's easier to just not try. But I think it's worth trying, if it helps the rising generation feel reassured about the true nature of their loving Heavenly Father and His plan for them, their families, and their loved ones.

Given the way we have taught the plan of salvation, it's no surprise that the visitor our stake presidency received in the introduction, felt that his calling entitled him to assess who might receive God's greatest gift of Eternal Life[72] and who might not. When we teach the rising generation to rely on the so-called certainties of their teachers, and when those certainties are passed down without challenge, entrenched mindsets encumber revealed doctrine. They become a barrier between the rising generation and God, instead of facilitating a revelatory relationship with Him.

Here is an example of what can happen:

In 2000, as I prepared to leave on my mission to Spain, I decided I wanted to have a handmade, laminated, colour diagram of the plan of salvation. Picture it in your mind; you know the one. I learned how to draw it in Primary. I planned to carry my diagram in my scriptures and use it as a visual aid to support my teaching. I remember drawing it, colouring it, cutting it out, laminating it, and cutting it out again. There was a white orb for the pre-mortal existence, a heavenly shower curtain for the veil, a well-drawn blue and green globe, a coffin to represent death, a cloud for spirit paradise, jail bars for spirit prison, an empty tomb for the resurrection, a judge's gavel for the Final Judgement and then a sun, a moon, and a star to represent the three kingdoms of glory. On the reverse of each component of my diagram, I wrote scripture references. On my mission, I used visual aids as often as I could. Not only that, but as a means of drawing people into a gathering crowd. Our more artistic elders and sisters would draw the

72 Doctrine and Covenants 14:7

same map in coloured chalks on the pavements of Spain. It looked like this:

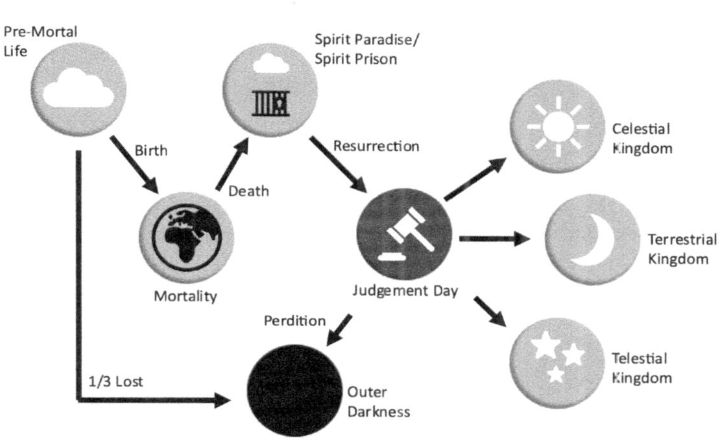

Figure 1

When I returned, matured, and gained exposure to ambiguity and the challenges that people face in their lives, I started to notice things about this diagram. I first noticed that it wasn't taught in our modern-day Church curricula. You won't find it in any of the updated manuals, *Come, Follow Me* or *Preach My Gospel*. Today it exists only on the internet, old lesson manuals, and in living memory. Yet you would be hard pressed to find a member of the Church (of any age) who can't quickly sketch it. It has become ubiquitous.[73]

I also noticed that although each component of the diagram could be referenced in some form or another in the scriptures, those same scriptures did not fully explain all of the interdependencies, sequencing, timing, or finality declared with certainty by the construction of the diagram. The role of the Saviour was minimal, absent even, and

73 At the time of publication, Preach My Gospel was amended to include a new image of the plan of salvation. We should ask ourselves why this has been drawn and what is now being emphasised.
Preach My Gospel: A Guide to Sharing the Gospel of Jesus Christ (Salt Lake City: The Church of Jesus Christ of Latter-day Saints), Gospel Library App.

the gaps between the component parts were being filled in with unrevealed assumptions.

Anecdotally, I noticed that instead of focusing on doctrines that had been revealed, this mental-map became positioned as a primary means to inform people's understanding of Heavenly Father's plan and by extension His nature. Because of its simplicity, it appealed to missionaries, children, and new converts. Its teaching proliferated quickly and not always in a helpful way. Said a friend:

> I grew up scared of God. I was taught in Primary that I had come to earth and that this life was my one shot at being with my family forever. When frustrated, my Dad would always remind us kids not to mess it up. I remember a fireside on family history and temple work for our ward. I don't remember the full script, as I was only seven. I do remember that I was dressed in white, playing the part of a deceased young girl who had not been sealed to her family. As I walked to the front, the person in charge told me that I could not enter the celestial kingdom and be with my family. Unable to tell the difference between the play and my reality, I was left traumatised. It was only later, when on my mission, that I started to ask myself "what happened to Jesus in the plan of salvation?" As I taught investigators about the repentance of the dead and proxy ordinances in the temple, I started to ask myself "if they can repent, why can't I?" I looked everywhere for answers to those questions.[74]

So how do we reassure the rising generation that there is space in the plan of salvation for their family members? How do we help them to have hope in Christ's mercy? How do we help them draw near to God and choose to believe in His goodness?

We can start by remembering that faith thrives in environments absent of certainty. Thinking and teaching that we must have a clear, unambiguous answer to every gospel question isn't how we set our hearts towards God, grow our faith, or build trust in Him. Regarding the plan of salvation, we can say with much more confidence we just

74 Personal Correspondence

don't have the answers to how it all works, but we can trust in the Father's true nature and stated intent to bring us home to Him.[75]

When our young people say "I don't know," it's not the end of faith but the beginning. By acknowledging Him and admitting that we don't have all the answers right now, we not only start in a more humble place, we signal to ourselves that we are open to receiving more as part of His ongoing restoration.[76] When we admit to not knowing something and still feel the desire to search, ponder, and pray, we leave mysteries open-ended which, in turn, enable more faith in God, more hope, and more charity towards ourselves and others.

By creating a space where we are comfortable with uncertainty, we can become more compassionate with those who find themselves struggling to fit the idealised templates of covenant-keeping families.

Because this diagram encapsulates so much of what we members believe, it can be hard to cope with the heartache felt from errant children expressing themselves, struggling, rebelling, or wandering lost. Not only is it painful when loved ones decide not to share the family faith, but the finality of their decision—and the associated psychological and emotional burdens—leave people fearful and trembling, instead of drawing hope from the Saviour.

Due to narratives culturally created from this diagram, people often assume that those who step back from practising their faith are lost, never to return to the eternal family meal table, making null and void the sealing ordinances they have received including the blessings of being born in the covenant.

The fear of 'empty chairs in heaven' means that when the rising generation want to stretch, explore, learn, or even rebel, the response from leaders, teachers, and parents is panic, clamping down, and holding on even more tightly. Often, contention builds and resentment grows. Under these pressures, families become fractured. The finality of a 'no second chances' narrative creates jeopardy and pain. For some, these tragic words from a friend are all too familiar:

---

75 Moses 1:39

76 LeGrand R. Curtis Jr, "The Ongoing Restoration." *Ensign 200 Years of Light: 1820-2020*. Salt Lake City, April 2020.

> I left the Church because I just couldn't keep up. Some days and weeks, I felt like I was on an expectations treadmill, set to maximum. Even though I knew that stepping off (or falling off) would have eternal consequences, which broke my mother's heart, I just couldn't do it anymore. We still don't talk.[77]

Consider our LGBTQ+ friends and members, and all of God's children who so identify. How do they fit into this diagram? How do they navigate the resulting tight spaces of their local faith experience, when this unreconcilable diagram stares back at them from the classroom walls of their childhood? Trying to force-fit this diagram and apply it to people's beautifully complex lives narrows the space and robs them of dignity, spiritual security, and psychological safety. That's not how Heavenly Father wants His children to feel. It's not what the Saviour taught to those who, deep down, desired to believe in Him.

Consider those members who are finding joy in making and striving to keep covenants, who belong to wonderful families that aren't visually aligned with the covenant path. The diagram of circles understandably leaves them asking "how can my family possibly fit into God's plan?"

Too many associate the plan of salvation with jeopardy, because of this diagram. Although we tried to revise the name to the plan of happiness, the underlying mindsets didn't really move at all.

Instead of being a welcoming Father, One whose work and glory is to bring us safely home,[78] One who enables us to be tested so that we can grow, and One who sent His beloved Son to rescue us from the wounds of the Fall and our own weakness, we fear Him as the One whose gavel will fall with a decree of banishment. Ultimately, the diagram values and emphasises justice far more than mercy or love.

The source of the diagram is no doubt D&C 76, but there are ambiguities in the revealed scriptures. Until further light and instruction come to make it all crystal clear, we can choose to act in faith and love God for what He has revealed and be generous with ourselves and others.

---

77 Personal Correspondence

78 Moses 1:39

With more comfort in not knowing, more trust in God, and more compassion for one another, we need to reconsider our ubiquitous diagram. If we feel we really do need a diagram, which we may not, we need to replace it with one that emphasises our journey home, with a focus on the rescuing atonement of Jesus Christ.

We shouldn't romantically fill-in gaps left in the scriptures or gaps not filled by restoration prophets, in an attempt to pacify those who struggle with the ambiguities the Lord has given us. Long term, that does their faith a disservice. But equally, we shouldn't leap to conclusions that haven't been revealed.

If the constructed narrative that we use to explain the plan of salvation existed on a pendulum, on one extreme we would have narrow certainties with no second chances and salvation dependent upon our knowledge and actions while the other side would hold an indifferent god who would save us no matter what. Neither of these extremes teach us or our youth to love or trust God. As members, we need to consider where along the path of the pendulum we should maintain the narrative and how we can incorporate the revealed truths of the atonement of Jesus Christ and the doctrine of repentance while not filling in for what the Lord has intentionally left out.

As we challenge the placement of the narrative pendulum, we are surely best served with the plan of salvation settled where the Lord has placed it, on the more neutral ground of "we don't know everything right now, as it hasn't been explicitly revealed." By letting it settle here, we create the needed space for people to feel hope, to love unconditionally, and to come unto Christ with confidence. We can trust that He will sort it all out and make it right in the end.

The reasonable question our young people grapple with is whether a soul continues to progress in the next life through faith in Jesus Christ and repentance. If we placed more weight on mercy, infinitely available to those who choose Him, or eventually return to choose Him, we might all panic less, judge one another less, and devote more time to loving and empathising with those who struggle. With this lens of mercy, many might find themselves pulled to God out of love instead of being pushed towards Him out of duty or fear.

In 1918, President Joseph F. Smith recorded a vision he received of the spirit world. His words were later canonised as Section 138 of the Doctrine and Covenants. In his vision he saw the "hosts of the dead, both small and great."[79] He saw the Saviour appear and declare "liberty to the captives who had been faithful."[80] He also noted that the Saviour did not go in person to those identified as "the wicked and disobedient who had rejected the truth."[81] Instead, He

> organized his forces and appointed messengers, clothed with power and authority, and commissioned them to go forth and carry the light of the gospel to them that were in darkness, even to all the spirits of men; and thus was the gospel preached to the dead. . . . even unto *all who would repent of their sins and receive the gospel.* Thus was the gospel preached to those who had died in their sins, without a knowledge of the truth, *or in transgression*, having rejected the prophets.[82]

It would appear that, in the most clear description that we have of the next life, the infinite atonement of Jesus Christ, the doctrines of repentance, and that of forgiveness endure. The arms of safety[83] remain open, and the prodigals among us who choose to come home through Christ will yet have their chance to be healed by Him.

By intentionally creating more space in the plan of salvation for all to rely on the Saviour, our radically inclusive young people will lead us beyond feelings of terror and insecurity at the thought of a loved one departing the faith or never subscribing to it in the first place. By us helping to remove the fear and the threat, they will more readily relax into a more confident and personally enriching faith journey to Him. Personal growth in His light and in His love would likely become their focus. The resulting space would likely give us all more motivation to live the two great commandments[84] and steer clear and grow out of the unjust judgement of others' journeys.

---

79 Doctrine and Covenants 138:11

80 Doctrine and Covenants 138:18

81 Doctrine and Covenants 138:29

82 Doctrine and Covenants 138:31-32 emphasis added

83 Alma 34:16

84 Matthew 22:36-40

This newfound focus would also increase trust in the power of ordinances that bind us to Christ and to each other. Imagine what could happen if the rising generation grew up learning to love a space-creating Christ whose eternal mercy, when enabled through faith in Him and repentance through Him, eventually helps us to meet the standards of the Father.

The obvious problem with a second chance narrative is that it sounds too much like Nephi's warning to those who want to "eat drink and be merry for tomorrow we die; . . . [H]e will justify in committing a little sin."[85] For some, a second chance narrative appears to ignore the teachings of Alma when he said "this life is the time to prepare to meet God."[86] Both of these scriptures used to be scripture mastery verses. Moreover, for many who were taught to cling tightly to the Fig 1 diagram and its resulting narratives, the natural reaction is "But what's the point, of all of this, if people can just repent later?" It's a good question. But not without prophetic answers.

Of course, questions remain around how accountable God will hold us for the ground in which we were planted, what level of light and truth we have truly received (as opposed to what we or others think we have received), and how He judges our mortal weakness, our failed best efforts, and the desires of our hearts. But the principle that this 'life is the time to prepare to meet God,' is not mutually exclusive with the idea that throughout this life and the next God will draw near to those that draw near to Him.

Consider these prophetic quotes that have received less local emphasis over the years, but that have the potential to chart a course towards a more faith filled middle ground while not sacrificing our core scriptural components.

Recalling that we will be made perfect in Christ, Joseph Smith taught

> When you climb up a ladder, you must begin at the bottom, and ascend step by step, until you arrive at the top; and so it is with the principles of the Gospel you must begin with the first, and go on until you

85 2 Nephi 28:7-8

86 Alma 34:32

> learn all the principles of exaltation. But it will be a *great while* after you have passed through the veil before you have learned them. It is not all to be comprehended in this world; it will be a great work to *learn* our salvation and exaltation even beyond the grave.[87]

Presumably such a *learning* environment includes making mistakes and presumably those mistakes can be corrected. Joseph also taught that "there is never a time when the soul is too old to approach God."[88]

Brigham Young said that "[those in lower kingdoms] would eventually have the privilege of proving themselves worthy of advancing to a celestial glory but it would be a slow process."[89]

Lorenzo Snow said "that sacrifice of the divine Being was effectual to destroy the powers of Satan. I believe that to every man and woman who comes into this life and passes through it, life will be a success in the end. It may not be in this life."[90]

President J. Reuben Clark wrote:

> I am not a strict constructionist, believing that we seal our eternal progress by what we do here. It is my belief that God will save all of His children that he can: and while, if we live unrighteous here, we shall not go to the other side in the same status, so to speak, as those who lived righteously; nevertheless, the unrighteous will have their chance, and in the eons of the eternities that are to follow, they, too, may climb to the destinies to which they who are righteous and serve God, have climbed.[91]

---

87 *Teachings of Presidents of the Church: Joseph Smith*, (Salt Lake City: The Church of Jesus Christ of Latter-day Saints, 2007), 268.

88 *History of the Church*, 4:425–26; from the minutes of a Church conference held on Oct. 3, 1841 in Nauvoo, Illinois, published in Times and Seasons, Oct. 15, 1841, 577–78.

89 Wilford Woodruff Journal, August 5, 1855, Wilford Woodruff journals and papers, 1828-1898, MS 1352, box 3, folder 1, Church History Library, https://catalog.churchofjesuschrist.org/assets/ed47e448-2936-4a1d-a4d8-4b5f96a8d1ac/0/72.

90 Lorenzo Snow Discourse, The Latter-day Saints' Millennial Star, LVI, no.4 (January 22, 1894), 52, https://catalog.churchofjesuschrist.org/assets/658923b4-0a68-4a39-bcc8-a83a1be68b25/0/3?lang=eng.

91 J. Reuben Clark, "President Clark Delivers Easter Address in Ensign Stake," Church News, April 23, 1960, https://catalog.churchofjesuschrist.org/assets/

Finally, President Boyd K. Packer recounted this experience, when on assignment with President Harold B. Lee.

> Early one morning he called me to come into his hotel room. He was sitting in his robe reading *Gospel Doctrine*, by President Joseph F. Smith (1838– 1918) and said "Listen to this! 'Jesus had not finished his work when his body was slain, neither did he finish it after his resurrection from the dead; although he had accomplished the purpose for which he then came to the earth, he had not fulfilled all his work. And when will he? Not until he has redeemed and saved *every son and daughter* of our father Adam that have been or ever will be born upon this earth to the end of time, except the sons of perdition. That is his mission.[92]

There are of course counter-balancing quotes that appear to disagree with the hope set out in the above paragraphs, and so, if we feel uncomfortable, perhaps the safest approach and most reassuring to all is to appeal to the First Presidency for clarification.

In response to this very question of eternal progress, the First Presidency released this statement via their secretary, first in 1952 and then again in 1965:

> The brethren direct me to say that the Church has never announced a definite doctrine upon this point. Some of the brethren have held that it was possible in the course of progression to advance from one glory to another, invoking the principle of eternal progression; others of the brethren have taken an opposite view. But as stated, the Church has never announced a definite doctrine on this point.[93]

---

fb9532f0-268a-4e22-8f54-387649c7411f/0/2?lang=eng.

92 Boyd K. Packer, *The Brilliant Morning of Forgiveness*, General Conference (Salt lake City: The Church of Jesus Christ of Latter-day Saints, October 1995), Gospel Library App.

93 Terryl L. Givens, "How Limited Is Postmortal Progression?," *Yet To Be Revealed: Open Questions in Latter-day Saint Theology*, BYU Studies Quarterly 60:3, Provo, 127. https://byustudies.byu.edu/article/how-limited-is-postmortal-progression/#footnote-024

Prophets admitting that they do not know what hasn't yet been revealed, and aren't prepared to speculate, is not only healthy for a faith tradition but instructive to members learning to trust God. As we consider our own understanding, we are right to give heed to prophets and "walk by faith and not by sight."[94] It really is okay to not settle the debate. In fact, for now, we cannot settle the debate. In the spirit of finding more breadth beyond our narrow certainties, we should consider looking to a new diagram to support everybody's personal progress.

Figure 2

Figure 2 gives us a more faith enabling, inclusive, and spacious plan of salvation diagram, designed to emphasise the law of mercy through Jesus Christ as the eternal satisfier of justice. And yes, I included fun artistic simplifications for Primary children.

As an aside, perhaps there is a flawed premise in the idea that we can reduce the eternal plan and the great mysteries of God into a flowchart comprising a series of circles and arrows. Maybe the rising generation don't need a diagram. It's possible that our trying to do just that in the past is what got us into trouble and drives some of the culture of certainty and in-group mindsets. Because Fig. 1 isn't in the scriptures,

94 2 Corinthians 5:7

we can empathetically redraft and not panic. For now, let's agree that having a diagram is better than having no diagram at all.

Figure 2 focuses the rising generation on what we know rather than what we don't know. The focus of the diagram is the Saviour. It focuses on the journey we have all undertaken from the presence of God, hoping and expecting that we will return to Him. There is no off-ramp and, hopefully, a much-reduced feeling of insecurity.

It shows us all as we travel through the realities of the Creation, the Fall, Christ's Atonement, and the resurrection. The basic truth is conveyed that we can all return to our heavenly home through Christ if we so choose. If we will turn to Him in faith preparing ourselves by repentance, we can return healed from our mortal probation, healed from our wounds, and rescued from the experience.

Again, if we need a diagram, let this diagram adorn the walls of our chapels, Primary, and youth classrooms. Let this more hopeful diagram fill our minds and let our hearts grow in empathy and love for all fellow travellers. Focusing our collective mindset more firmly on the deep desire our heavenly parents have to see us return will help everyone feel more hopeful and more faith-filled.

For those who remain unconvinced, I find it difficult to reconcile the Lord's purpose to eventually bring all of God's children safely home to the stark mathematics of mortality. As Patrick Mason observed, if we assume that only the most faithful Latter-day Saints are headed to the celestial kingdom (as did our stake visitor in the opening training meeting), it can be hard to believe that the plan of salvation is a success. On the implied mathematics alone, the casualty rate from the more hard-line view of the plan is, at best, 99.8%.[95] Even if we assume that all baptised members of The Church of Jesus Christ of Latter-day Saints currently alive today 'make it back' (with zero attrition), the success rate of the plan for those alive on earth today would be less than two tenths of one percent. With 17 million baptised members in the world, we make up only two tenths of one percent of the

95 Patrick Q Mason, *Restoration: God's Call to the 21st-Century World*, (Meridian: Faith Matters Publishing, 2020), 41.

currently estimated global population, 8 billion.[96] Take the 33.3% acknowledged casualty rate from the War in Heaven, combine it with the 99.8% casualty rate from the War on Earth, and with the more hard-line view one must surely conclude that the celestial kingdom is a very quiet and lonely place.

The plan of salvation must surely be much, much more inclusive. And temple work isn't the point here. That's the answer to a different question (how do people who didn't receive saving ordinances in mortality also receive them?) No, something else must be going on, something altogether more generous. It is the generosity of a loving Heavenly Father that we should emphasise when validating the diversity of familial circumstances.

All diagrams aside, the language and imagery often associated with the plan of salvation, specifically the Final Judgement leads some of our young members within the Church to envision a courtroom, a Judge ready to find us wanting, ready to bang the gavel, and ready to banish us to a distant realm potentially away from our loved ones. This devastating read of the plan frames their understanding of the nature of their Heavenly Father and sows subtle seeds of distrust and fear. Those emotions are entirely inadequate as a platform on which to build faith and devotion.

We are all familiar with the inside of a courtroom: there is a witness box, space for the jury, and the clerk. There is space for the legal professionals to make their respective and competing cases. Perhaps there is a mezzanine gallery or an observation deck open to members of the press and public. In the courtroom, the defendant sits in the dock, alone, isolated, most likely intimidated and afraid. And above it all, raised at a higher level, sits the imposing figure of the judge. Once the drama of the courtroom has peaked, the defence has been heard, the prosecution has rested and the jury's verdict returned, the judge customarily brings down the gavel to indicate its binding finality. For the rising generation, the imagery of the Final Judgement can be merciless and exclusionary. Part of their struggle is because the scriptures use the same metaphor.

---

96 U.S. and World Populations Clock. United States Census Bureau. census.gov/popclock/ November 29th, 2023.

In the Book of Mormon, Jacob wrote:

> Know ye not that if ye will [deny] these things, that the power of the redemption and the resurrection, which is in Christ, will bring you to stand with shame and awful guilt before the bar of God? And according to the power of justice, for justice cannot be denied, ye must go away into that lake of fire and brimstone.[97]

When these outcomes are positioned by members as the destination of our best efforts, or the best efforts of our loved ones, it's no wonder that our young people often feel a sense of spiritual insecurity and sometimes a sense of terror with regards to how their family fits into the plan of salvation. Even their best efforts may not feel good enough, given the terrible outcomes that may await them or their family. But we don't need to panic.

In my own extended family (by birth and by marriage), there are some who have, for now, stepped back from the tradition of faith. Each has their own story. Each is loved without caveat or condition, and not because there is an expectation that they will one day return and repent. They are on their own journey to an all-powerful, all-healing, and all-loving eternal Saviour, who understands them perfectly as their Creator, Messiah, and Judge. Within the framework of temple sealings, we have confidence in Him and in the ultimate goodness of our family. We choose not to panic.

In my service, I have met with families torn apart by grief with relationships that have broken down and currently seem irreparable. Many of them live with the terror that comes from not knowing how the family will fit together in the eternities. Moreover, in my work with our young people, I have witnessed far too many instances of parents creating uncomfortable emotional spaces for their children as they struggle to maintain their best.

But who determines what somebody's best is? In my own life, my 'best' has meant different things at different times. I strive to be humble and to be faithful, but some Sundays I go to church fully equipped and ready to sing, teach, and testify while other times I get there look-

---

97 Jacob 6:9-10

ing for respite and relief. And sometimes I just can't wait to get home. Spending time in each of these spaces, feels like a normal experience.

Jacob and others like him describe the outcomes that await us if we are exposed to the full weight of the law of justice. He addresses those without any inclination or desire to exercise faith in Jesus Christ or to repent through Him. He is speaking about those with zero regard for Christ and those who completely and utterly reject His outstretched hand, stubbornly refusing to change their minds (until they do).

As a faith tradition, we've been effective at emphasising the justice elements of God's eternal laws, as captured in Fig 1. People got the message – get it wrong, wander off (or never join) the covenant path and these arrows will point you (or your loved ones) to a subordinated, poorly-lit, realm where you will live alone forever. We've been less effective at teaching the elements of His grace and mercy. Today we need to carry the message of Jesus Christ and His restorative healing powers into the local experience of the rising generation. These are also found in the scriptures.

In contrast to Jacob's warnings, his son Enos wrote:

> And soon I go to the place of my rest, which is in my Redeemer; for I know that in him I shall rest. And I rejoice in the day when my mortal shall put on immortality, and shall stand before him; then shall I see his face with pleasure, and he will say unto me: Come unto me, ye blessed, there is a place prepared for you in the mansions of my Father. Amen.[98]

Enos looked forward to the Final Judgement with joy and rejoicing. He knew it would be a pleasurable experience. In his spiritual projection, Enos felt that, in that heavenly moment, the Lord would invite Him (and not banish him) to come unto Him. Enos also felt that He would choose to go with him because He had learned to love Him by keeping the commandments.

President Uchtdorf taught:

> After the Resurrection, there will be a Day of Judgment. . . . That Day of Judgment will be a day of mercy and love—a day when broken

98 Enos 1:27

> hearts are healed, when tears of grief are replaced with tears of gratitude, when all will be made right.[99]

As leaders, teachers, and parents, let's replace the threatening courtroom and the judge's gavel as imagery for the Final Judgment. We might instead use an analogy of an old hotel, where behind the reception desk neatly hang seemingly infinite individual room keys. Each key leads to a room that has been prepared and made up. There is a room for everybody. No exceptions. Our loving Heavenly Father earnestly wants us to come to the hotel, to announce ourselves at the reception desk, and to claim our key. There is a key (and a room) for each of our family members, our friends, strangers in the street, and of course for us, no matter what our mortal experiences have made us feel about ourselves.

In this metaphor, the act of collecting our key represents coming unto Jesus Christ, through faith and repentance and restoration through the covenants and ordinances of His gospel.

Over the years, some taught that the hotel stays open 24/7 throughout all eternity, offering a universally stretched-out hand of invitation to all. Ultimately, they felt that everybody who kept their first estate would have an eternal opportunity to change their heart, come unto Him, and start, or restart, their journey towards collecting their key. Others taught that the hotel had a closing time and that ultimately there would, by extension, be many keys that would be eternally uncollected.

Remember, we don't know the exact schedule of the hotel. But not knowing isn't a weakness; it's a strength. The not knowing creates space for hope, for love, for empathy for family and friends, trusting that they really do fit into God's plan. The hotel analogy creates room for more faith and trust in God our Father and His Only Begotten Son, Jesus Christ.

By teaching the rising generation an updated plan of salvation diagram, one that includes only what the Lord has revealed, we can help

---

99 Dieter F. Uchtdorf, *O How Great the Plan of Our God!*, General Conference (Salt Lake City: The Chruch of Jesus Christ of Latter-day Saints, October 2016), Gospel Library App.

them to prioritise their personal growth in their searching, pondering, and praying. With a more generous mind map, we can help them find more space to keep the two great commandments and trust that God will do what He has said He will do. The real miracle of the hotel metaphor is that the hotel has been built. The work is done. The keys are cut and the rooms are ready. And the owner of the hotel has said that it is His job (His work and His glory) to target one hundred percent occupancy.

Chapter Summary

Many within the rising generation don't feel confident that their families are represented or included in the narrow presentation of the plan of salvation that they learned in Primary. This often causes a feeling of perceived threat from the Final Judgement.

Creating Space for Christ the Healer

"I feel shame when I make mistakes – not hope. It makes me want to give up."

Alicia, 19

A FRIEND WROTE:

> I left the Church, in my early twenties. Ten years on, I now find myself living as an active Christian, largely because of who I married. My husband and I are raising our two children, with the support of our local village church. We have a good community spirit and the vicar is sweet-natured. Every Sunday, he teaches about the life of Christ and expands just a few verses of the Bible that detail His love and healing nature. He then finds a way to link us to Him as our personal Saviour. The genuine love our vicar has for his small flock makes me want to be better. I really do look forward to his messages. I can honestly say that I don't resent the LDS Church, in fact I'm grateful to it. I didn't realise how much I knew about Christianity until I joined another congregation. Funnily enough, I still pray like a Mormon. I also hold the same commitment in my heart to the doctrines of the Creation, the Fall, and the Atonement. But in this new space, I feel less burdened. I have reflected on why I left many times. It ultimately comes down to this: my Mormon faith felt too disconnected from Christ. I felt the priority was for me to live somebody else's life. Maybe somebody in Utah, I'm not sure. All I knew was that it was a life of high expectations, high achievement, and high performance. It

> was exhausting. My callings often felt busier than my actual job as a nurse. I just didn't see my life reflected in the stories, realities, or anecdotes shared so casually in manuals and talks from the top. It created real pressure in my life, which I handled only because that pressure was less than the guilt I knew I would feel were I to leave. Once the guilt started to wear away, perhaps as I got older, I made my decision to step back. By then I wasn't really living all the standards anyway, so it became easier to justify. I still have lots of friends who are members, and I haven't turned into a hater or a troll. But all they seem to want to talk about is how the Church needs to change, or how busy they are in their callings. I often come away from those exchanges feeling a mixture of sadness and gratitude. If I try and turn the conversation to Christ, they think I'm being a bit preachy.[100]

Feeling more connected to the expectations of others, as opposed to Christ Himself, is a feeling held in common by many of the young people I speak with. Although their programmes and activities are different, they echo the generation of programmes that came before where the focus is centred on goals, activity, and achievement. These goals, activities, and achievements create in-groups of high-performers.

As a young man of the 1990s, I experienced a keen emphasis on *doing* via a variety of programmes including Duty to God and the Scouting programme with their many tasks, goals and badges. Moreover, I observed my sisters work through their Personal Progress with its various chapters and achievements, ribbons, and pendants. Doubtless these programmes were tied to a life of faith in Jesus Christ, but when those linkages were overlooked in favour of filling up activities including mutual nights and summer camps, it's no surprise that many later struggle with feelings of not being good enough. Today, these patterns and feelings continue to exist amongst many of our young people. When we add the mindsets portrayed in the prior chapter, it's understandable why feelings of scrupulosity take hold.

Today there appear to be many who want the focus of our young people to be on high expectations and high achievements, made possible by the extraordinary depth of talent and resources available where the Church is well established. However, when these habits and expec-

100 Personal Correspondence

tations are exported to international congregations where the skills and resources are much thinner and where, at times, the Saviour's healing disappears from the narrative, church can get hard. And when church gets hard, faith gets hard.

Excitingly, changes are coming. We are undoubtedly becoming more Christ-centred. These changes are happening from the top, but, as is always the case, they take time to filter down to the local experience. One example of these changes is clear and concerted effort the Church has made to drop the nickname 'Mormons,' reminding us to use the full name of the Church which bears the name of Jesus Christ. Another, perhaps more subtle example, is the reminder to avoid removing the Mediator from our teachings and choice of language. Said President Nelson:

> There is no amorphous entity called "the Atonement" upon which we may call for succor, healing, forgiveness, or power. Jesus Christ is the source. Sacred terms such as *Atonement* and *Resurrection* describe what the Savior did, according to the Father's plan, so that we may live with hope in this life and gain eternal life in the world to come. The Savior's atoning sacrifice—the central act of all human history—is best understood and appreciated when we expressly and clearly connect it to Him.[101]

By refocusing our young people on Jesus Christ and their personal connection to Him, they will undoubtedly find a less encumbered and more sustaining path to Him. As local leaders, teachers, and parents, we can support these changes. But it's not just about them being connected to Him, it's about them being connected to Him as their personal Healer.

Consider the below graph showing the number of references to Christ as our healer made at general conference since the 1850s.

---

101 Russell M. Nelson, *Drawing the Power of Jesus Christ into Our Lives*, General Conference (Salt Lake City: The Church of Jesus Christ of Latter-day Saints, April 2017), Gospel Library App.

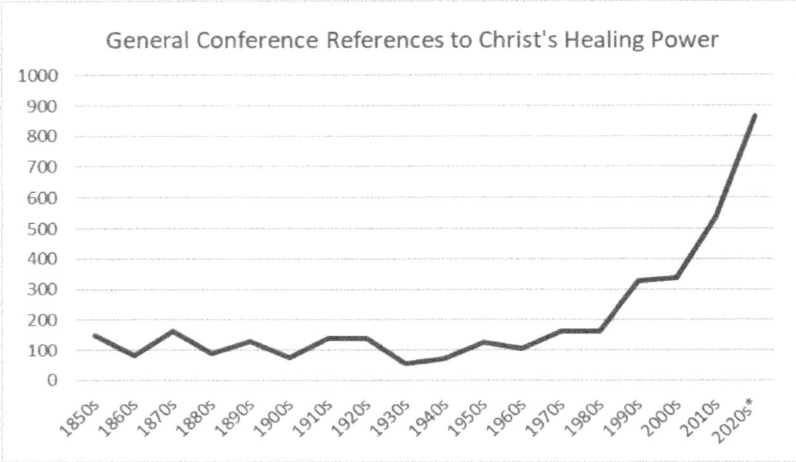

(2020s data extrapolated for full decade)

We might ask ourselves what we can learn, and how we might align our local teaching styles to this growing trend. Although the above chart has been extrapolated to the end of the 2020s, it's clear that in the 2010s references to Christ's healing power or identity as our Healer increased almost five hundred percent when compared to prior decades.[102]

Elder Holland said, "'*Come as you are*,' a loving Father says to each of us, but He adds, 'Don't plan to stay as you are.' We smile and remember that God is determined to make of us more than we thought we could be."[103]

We want our young people to choose to come unto Christ and then to be transformed by Him as they are sanctified beyond their current state, through His healing power. This transformation by Him will lead to them choosing to abide with Him, living by His commandments not out of duty but out of love. But to help them feel motivated by the idea of such a transformation, we need to connect them to

---

102 This graph was created using that data made available on www..lds-general-conference.org

103 Jeffrey R. Holland, *Songs Sung and Unsung*, General Conference (Salt Lake City: The Church of Jesus Christ of Latter-day Saints, April 2017), Gospel Library App.

Him. To do this well at the local level, there are four things we can prioritise.

Firstly, we can redefine success in the gospel. Secondly, we can connect our young people to the beauty of their individual weakness. Thirdly, we can continue to remove the stigma around repentance. And fourthly, we can help them find connection in their best efforts at worthiness.

I recently asked a family member for her definition of success, within the context of her faith. She said:

> For me, success is personal growth by coming unto Jesus Christ. It's not serving a mission or getting married in the temple – although that seems to be what we mostly teach our young men and young women. Success is not an eternal family of lifelong active children or serving in a crescendo of busy and prominent callings. Of course, I see the value in these things and I would want them for everybody. But I am successful when I grow, allowing Christ to heal and transform me through His healing power. And I could substitute 'grow' with 'make mistakes, repent, and try again.' I think of it this way: if I were to ask my home ward to all stand up one Sunday morning, and then invite them to sit down if they are married in the temple, with all their children active in the faith, it's true that a number of them would sit down. Wonderful. But most, in my experience, would be left standing. Would this make them failures in their faith? Of course not. And yet so many feel this way. For me success is achieved when we personally grow by coming unto Jesus Christ. The covenant path is not one single covenant path for all of God's children (although it can easily be taught this way) but rather a personal covenant path that leads to personal growth and transformation in Him. Of course, this may lead us to serving a mission, marrying in the temple, getting a degree and . . . and . . . and . . . but it also might not.[104]

If we could establish success as personal growth by coming unto Christ, we would establish the Saviour as the focus of our young people's faith experience. We would also more readily support our young people in connecting to Him personally and transforming into dis-

104 Personal Correspondence

ciples who choose Him again and again. What's more – such a definition of success is one hundred percent inclusive. Everybody can achieve personal growth in this way, through big steps and small steps, irrespective of their starting points and their personal circumstances. Returning to the above hypothetical, when asking those who were successful to sit down, nobody would be left standing.

The second local reframing we could share with our young people is not only that Christ heals them from their weakness, but that their weakness is part of the plan. In the Book of Ether, Moroni recorded this revelation, with emphasis added:

> And if men come unto me I will show unto them their *weakness*. I give unto men *weakness* that they may be humble; and my grace is sufficient for all men that humble themselves before me; for if they humble themselves before me, and have faith in me, then will I make weak things become strong unto them.[105]

Over the years, I have seen this scripture be positioned as a reminder to overcome idiosyncratic shortcomings, a lack of skills, or even a personality flaw. But Moroni is teaching us much more than learning to control our tempers, or to be less cynical, or to have a stronger memory.

For me, he is reminding us that we are designed with weakness. The plan has weakness hard-coded in. Weakness should not cause discouragement, frustration, or depression. Weakness should not trigger feelings of scrupulosity. Weakness is to be expected, even celebrated. It creates our own personal base-line from which we grow and transform though Him.

I saw this taught masterfully by a sister in our ward one Sunday. She called her lesson The Parable of the Cabbage. As she stood at the front of her class, she held a beautiful, leafy green cabbage. She explained:

> In the centre of the cabbage rests its heart. Surrounding this heart are the cabbage leaves, which have grown in overlapping layers to give the vegetable its form, its size, and its beauty. The heart can be found by

---

105 Ether 12:27

> peeling off the leaves, one at a time. But the leaves aren't wasted. The leaves are the cabbage; the cabbage is its leaves.
>
> The cabbage represents each of us. We all have many experiences and circumstances beyond our control, linked to our starting points and our places of planting. All of these need healing from our Saviour.
>
> Take me for example, when I was in my mother's womb, her addictions had a lasting impact on me. Today I have real struggles that took me a long time to understand.
>
> As she said this, she removed a layer of the cabbage and placed it on the table.
>
> As a child, I experienced certain traumas that I've wrestled with in therapy. I've come to realise that some of the mindsets I have about myself have their anchors in those early moments.
>
> Again, she removed a layer of the cabbage and placed it on the table.
>
> I sometimes burn out when I serve because I learned to be a perfectionist, when I was younger. I was eager to please my parents, especially when they were going through their divorce.
>
> She removed another leaf.
>
> Fast forward to today and I'm a huge people-pleaser. Sometimes this leads me to do things I later regret.
>
> Another leaf.

She continued through the demonstration. With every honest and insightful comment about her life, her choices, experiences outside of her control, even those seemingly within her control, she removed a leaf. She explained how sometimes her choices and her 'sins' seemed to come from a place of insecurity, a feeling of brokenness. At times, they were compensations for anxiety, frustration and even loneliness. She described her sins as her wounds. She pointed out that what some called a sinful nature, others called a wounded soul.

Eventually, as her empathic teaching and self-deprecating sense of humour brought her to the heart of the cabbage. She asked someone to read a scripture from the Doctrine and Covenants:

"For I, the Lord will judge all men according to their works, according to the desire of their hearts."[106]

---

106 Doctrine and Covenants 137:9

She then bore a powerful testimony of how grateful she was for her weakness, for her Saviour's healing power and her continuing (and at times slow) transformation into her best, celestial self. She shared her gratitude for how she was learning to overcome her challenges with faith, humility, and good works. She shared how she created space for her to be judged on her desires, even if sometimes her desires didn't translate immediately into what she hoped they would. As for the cabbage leaves, she didn't dismiss them as unimportant. She recognised that she was being led to what Christ wanted her to become through His healing and His love, not in spite of her weakness but because of it.

Her parable is not unlike the altogether more generous interpretation of *sin*, put forward in *All Things New* by Terryl and Fiona Givens.

> Seeing our condition as wounded is a spur to charity rather than to judgement. The impact of seeing the "sinner" as the "wounded" is profound and meaningful in the here and now. This perspective is not an abstract theological prescription but a recipe for a more vibrant and caring discipleship in the present world. In the Christian past, sin was equated with a contagion. Even now, hearing that a person is mired in sin, we tend to label, to retreat, to avoid, to shun. If we hear instead that the individual is deeply wounded, our heart is drawn out in compassion, and our inclination is to succour and heal. Categories like "the saved" and "the damned," and "the righteous," erect boundaries and invite judgment. Recognising the universality of our woundedness and the universal love of God invites community and mutual concern.[107]

The third means of creating more space for Christ the Healer among our young people is to remove all stigmas from the repentance process. Thankfully, this is also an area that has been identified for improvement at General Conference. President Nelson taught:

> The word for *repentance* in the Greek New Testament is *metanoeo*. The prefix *meta-* means "change." The suffix *-noeo* is related to Greek

107 Fiona Givens and Terryl Givens, *All Things New: Rethinking Sin, Salvation, and Everything in Between*, (Meridian: Faith Matters Publishing, 2020), 108.

> words that mean "mind," "knowledge," "spirit," and "breath." Thus, when Jesus asks you and me to "repent," He is inviting us to change our mind, our knowledge, our spirit—even the way we breathe. He is asking us to change the way we love, think, serve, spend our time, treat our wives, teach our children, and even care for our bodies.[108]

As local leaders, teachers, and parents, we should ask ourselves why the living prophets are teaching us to normalise the doctrine of repentance and forgiveness. Removing cultural connotations of shame that have become attached to repentance helps all of us, but it especially helps the rising generation. Importantly, the prophet didn't remove the requirements for us all to repent; nor did he downplay the significance of coming unto Christ. Instead, he encouraged us to evolve and transition our understanding away from punishment and towards the open arms of Jesus.

In the same general conference talk, he taught:

> Too many people consider repentance as punishment—something to be avoided except in the most serious circumstances. But this feeling of being penalized is engendered by Satan. He tries to block us from looking to Jesus Christ, who stands with open arms, hoping and willing to heal, forgive, cleanse, strengthen, purify, and sanctify us. . . . Nothing is more liberating, more ennobling, or more crucial to our individual progression than is a regular, daily focus on repentance. Repentance is not an event; it is a process. It is the key to happiness and peace of mind. When coupled with faith, repentance opens our access to the power of the Atonement of Jesus Christ.[109]

For the rising generation, understanding His healing nature places their journeys of faith into the empowering context of traveling home to a concerned, loving God who wants to heal them from their weakness. It allows them to confidently own their starting point, as well as their personal headwinds. As repentance is normalised, they are able to travel with more authenticity and success.

---

108 Russell M. Nelson, *We Can Do Better and Be Better*, General Conference (Salt Lake City: The Church of Jesus Christ of Latter-day Saints, April 2019), Gospel Library App.

109 Ibid

The fourth and final suggestion to support the rising generation connect to Christ the Healer is to help them connect when they are struggling with their own understanding of worthiness.

When we stop to think about how the youth experience shame, it is usually because their private repentance has been brought into a public space. This might be when young people confess their sins to a third party, such as the bishop, or when they face sanctions as part of their repentance process.

Bishops do important work, in their roles as the Lord's appointed judges in Israel. They create confessional space in the Church, helping members to reset their relationships with God. They don't forgive sins. Only God does that. But they can help members find joy in their covenants, in how they teach about the healing powers of Jesus Christ. There is value in having a physical representative of the Saviour that you can speak to and interact with. That said, bishops are also lay, volunteer ministers. Our bishops are bankers, lawyers, factory workers, schoolteachers, doctors, academics, policemen, and entrepreneurs. They bring their backgrounds and their understanding to the position. Bishops make mistakes and do their best. These realities can lead to very different experiences for our youth and young adults.

Consider the following two fictional abstractions that highlight how shame can unnecessarily enter the repentance process and unintentionally disconnect people from Christ the Healer. Firstly, Miguel who sets an appointment to speak with his bishop about the law of chastity.

> Miguel looked at something he felt he shouldn't have and did something he felt he shouldn't have. Deep down in his heart he felt he knew better. Into his mind poured the scriptural passages that he had learned in seminary, his Aaronic Priesthood lessons, talks at church, and family nights. "No unclean thing can dwell"[110] with God; "wickedness never was happiness;"[111] "the Spirit of the Lord is grieved, . . . Amen to the priesthood of that man;"[112] "whoso eateth and drinketh my flesh and blood un-

110 Moses 6:57

111 Alma 41:10

112 Doctrine and Covenants 121:37

worthily eateth and drinketh damnation to his soul."[113] He felt ashamed. Wanting to "put things right with the Lord," in his words, he found the courage to book an appointment with his bishop.

During the appointment, Bishop Pasado opened the scriptures and read about the Saviour. Miguel listened. Bishop did his best to reassure him. Without asking Miguel many questions, the bishop prescribed a short period of abstaining from the sacrament. Miguel was told not to prepare, pass, or administer and told not to partake of the emblems for a few weeks. During that prescribed period, they agreed to stay in touch by phone call, appointment, and text message. There was a youth temple trip coming up and unfortunately, he would have to sit it out. Miguel decided to keep it quiet and manage his feelings of embarrassment by telling his family that he felt unwell. On Sunday, he dreaded going to church. He hoped that his parents, younger siblings, and fellow young men wouldn't notice that he didn't pass the sacrament and that he didn't partake when the trays were passed to his family's row. Although they generously pretended not to notice, they did, and he knew it. He felt disconnected and ashamed. His exclusion reinforced his family and friends' own misaligned understanding of the doctrine of repentance. A few weeks later, the young man's time ran down, he met once more with Bishop Pasado and the sanctions were lifted. The bishop felt good that he had helped one of his youth; the young man eventually felt better and moved on. Deep down, however, Miguel felt anxiety and shame. He came to associate those feelings with the Atonement of Jesus Christ and the Church. He struggled as a teenager and continued his transactional repentance with his bishop, each time taking the prescription of exclusion. Eventually, his unresolved shame and his reality of coming unto His bishop and not unto Christ left him feeling disconnected. In time, he left the Church, although he never stopped believing in God.

It wasn't Bishop Pasado's intention for Miguel to feel shamed but there was no connection to Christ and the sacrament used as a punish-

113 3 Nephi 18:29

ment had this effect. Contrast this experience with that of Sofia and Bishop Cambio:

> Sofia is also struggling with the law of chastity. She too feels ashamed and is prayerfully, even desperately, trying to repent. She broke up with her boyfriend, who doesn't share her faith, and resolved to not date so intensively until she is older. She found setting boundaries difficult when trying to find love and to feel loved.
>
> Sofia is trying to listen to more spiritually uplifting music and reading the scriptures more regularly. When she reads the Young Women's theme which hangs above her bed, she feels like nothing will lift her shame.
>
> She too has a temple trip coming up and is terrified of her father learning that she won't be able to go inside. She is from a strong church family, and there are clear expectations from her parents on how the gospel should be lived. Not knowing what to do, she buries her head in the sand. A spiritual depression begins to take hold. She feels numb inside but is able to fake it so that nobody around her suspects anything.
>
> At her midweek mutual evening, she is at the chapel with her friends. Bishop Cambio is also there. His plan is to spend five minutes with each of the youth to ensure temple recommends haven't expired and that everybody is able to participate. Sofia's recommend expired recently. He pops his head into the Young Women's activity and invites her for a quick catch up.
>
> After an opening prayer, he warmly asks how she is getting on. Sofia explains what has happened through her tears.
>
> Bishop Cambio is loving, empathic, and reassuring. He bears a simple and short testimony of the Saviour's mercy and endless love for her. He respectfully explores her feelings and ministers to her emotional distress. He meets her where she is at and slowly moves the interview on after she has been heard and is ready. He reminds her that nobody is perfect and that weakness is part of the plan. Although this is a heavy burden, he reminds her that she was never meant to carry it alone. He asks her open-ended

questions that strengthen her understanding of the Saviour's love and acceptance of her best efforts.

He knows to connect her to the Source and is careful not to connect her to him as the bishop. His focus is to help her come unto Christ and have experiences with Him.

He asks if she would like a blessing, knowing that great power can come into her life through the ordinance of a blessing. She accepts. In the blessing, He avoids giving her advice and starts most of his sentences with "I bless you with . . ." and "I bless you that . . ."

He invites her to participate in the ordinance of the sacrament that coming Sunday, so that she can feel the power of her Saviour's mercy, as she connects her repentance to Him through His holy ordinance.

Bishop Cambio sets her some light homework – to find and reflect upon three verses of scripture that help her feel closer to Jesus Christ. He invites her to come and share those with him after church on Sunday. Finally, together, they read a couple of short scriptures, to help orientate her. Bishop Cambio reads one and Sofia reads the other. She marks them in her phone.

Sunday comes and Sofia has what she will later describe as her first real spiritual experience. She feels loved. She feels supported. She feels connected to Christ through the binding ordinance of the sacrament. She meets with Bishop Cambio again. She shares her scriptures and again feels the love of the Saviour.

He signs her recommend, encourages her to prepare spiritually for the temple, and expresses his love for her. Sofia cannot understand how it has all turned around so quickly. Her guilt has been swept away. Two Sundays later, Bishop Cambio invites her to share her testimony with the ward members about her experience at the temple. Sofia does so and bears a powerful testimony of the Saviour and feels full of gratitude. Her parents and ward members are touched by the power of her faith, and everybody goes home feeling changed.

> Bishop Cambio continues to check in with her, not to observe or monitor her choices, but to ensure that she feels supported, sustained, and motivated in her faith.

What would happen to those visiting the bishop's office if we as leaders, teachers, and parents modelled the behaviours and attitudes of Bishop Cambio? What sort of relationship would they develop with repentance as they progress into adulthood? What a blessing it would be to the rising generation when trying to find Christ the Healer. Beautifully, as he represents and models the Saviour's love for them, Bishop Cambio teaches our young people that repentance is among the most sweet and joyful experiences they can have.

Although we review Bishop Pasado with love and generosity, when our young people are repentant and hopeful that He will heal their wounded souls, they need connection not disconnection. Bishop Cambio creates connection that encourages love and further repentance.

The rising generation do not have to be flawless to be worthy or to connect with God. Their worthiness comes from their love of God, their desire to return to Him and their best efforts.

We need to teach them that only God forgives and heals us from our wounds and weakness. It is God who looketh upon our hearts and it is only God who knows what He finds there. It doesn't mean that we don't have to sincerely turn and return to Him. But it does mean that we can challenge any local cultures that disconnect our youth from the Saviour and instead more closely align ourselves to the doctrine of repentance and forgiveness.

In the Book of Mormon, we read these three short verses, with emphasis added:

> Yea, I would that ye would come forth and harden not your hearts any longer; for behold, now it the time and the day of your salvation; and therefore, if ye will repent and harden not your hearts, *immediately* shall the great plan of redemption be brought about unto you.[114]

---

114 Alma 34:31

> Fear not for thou shalt not be ashamed, . . . for thou shalt not be put to shame; for *thou shalt forget the shame of thy youth* and shalt not remember the reproach of thy youth.[115]

> God will be merciful unto many; and *our children shall be restored*, that they may come to that which will give them the true knowledge of their Redeemer.[116]

When repentance is sincere, great power comes into our lives as we seek to draw strength and power from the Lord through His ordinances. In the ordinances of the priesthood, "the power of godliness is manifest."[117] When our young people repent, the Saviour wants them to feel loved and connected, not isolated. He wants them to have opportunities to feel a greater portion of His healing power. He wants them to be brought closer to the restorative powers and true knowledge of their Redeemer.

During His ministry, Jesus heals the blind, the lame, the leprous, and the dumb. He heals the possessed, the deaf, the diseased, the afflicted, the smitten, the downtrodden, and the weary. He heals those who believe in Him and those who struggle with reservations and doubts. He heals those who do all they can to draw near to Him and He heals those who literally need to be carried to Him by others. He heals those who ask Him for help and those whose family members appeal on their behalf.

As we teach the rising generation to seek Christ the Healer and connect them with the beauty of their divinely-given weakness, they will be able to build momentum through connecting to Him and repent with more confidence. These various messages are being taught with clarity by the prophets and general leaders of the Church. It's up to us as local leaders to help them become more firmly established within the local experience of our young people.

---

115 3 Nephi 22:4

116 2 Nephi 10:2

117 Doctrine and Covenants 84:20

Chapter Summary

Many of our young people say they struggle to find the healing Christ in their church experience.

We can help them feel excited by the personal transformation that comes from feeling healed by Him, as we shift the emphasis from His judgement to His grace.

Creating Space for the Kingdom of God

I love the gospel and feel comfortable when I feel God's love, but church life feels harder than I think it should. I would like to think I can hold onto my faith in God, but I'm not completely sure I can see myself as an 'active' member of the Church when I get older. It would really depend on a lot of things.

Kia, 16

I BELIEVE WE MAKE IT DIFFICULT FOR THE RISING GENERATION WHEN we only share our strongest moments. If everybody only shares their personal highlight reel in sacrament talks and Sunday lessons, our young people can become convinced that faith in Christ means constant revelation, burnings in the bosom, and flawlessly keeping covenant commitments. When everybody around them takes this approach, our faith tradition becomes an uncomfortable and narrowing space for them, especially as their lives become more complex.

Authentic reminders that life doesn't travel in straight lines and that sometimes, even when we do our best to follow Christ, we find ourselves "in a dark and dreary waste,"[118] can be both reassuring and

118 1 Nephi 8:7

space-creating. Nowhere is this more true than when the things we share show how Christ brings us through such times.

There was a time in my life when I wasn't sure how I felt about my faith. I always believed in and loved Jesus Christ and never wandered from Him, but during this particular time, I felt tired and stretched beyond my capacity. Instead of finding joy in the gospel, at times I found frustration with my experiences as a member of the Church.

A year and a half after getting married, I was called to serve as the bishop and Jen was called to serve in the Stake Young Women's presidency. We were 24 years old.

At this young age, we didn't realise it at the time but our religious expression was mostly defined by our sense of duty towards Church callings. Our callings helped us to feel connected to the Church but not necessarily always to the Saviour.

After being called, I was warmly invited into people's homes. Almost immediately, I began to see how complicated their lives were despite their good choices and strong faith. In short, my service exposed my privilege and showed me where my outlook on life and people had become narrow.

I learned first-hand that people's challenges came from their starting points, their circumstances, and the choices of others beyond their control.

As I began to spend more time in counsel with members of the ward, and as their trust for me increased, they began to share their faith struggles. In each case, our members had personal and private struggles around questions to which they couldn't find satisfactory answers. One shared his frustrations with race and the priesthood and would bring his research and findings to our meetings. Another would share her concerns around Church history and patriarchy in particular. Many shared their traumas from how their parents had taught the gospel in their homes, with their parents holding fast to what my members felt were narrow and exclusionary teachings. I had members who identified as LGBTQ+ who were desperately holding onto faith and feeling let down by the tone and teachings of the Church. I also sat with members who had endured various forms of abuse and continued to struggle with the resulting trauma, asking "where was God, during my darkest moments?" No one story was the same. Their faith was fragile but they kept coming, kept loving, and kept serving. I recall one particular week where I had no fewer than five married couples come to me asking for help as they contemplated divorce. It was a heavy load.

In no time at all, these wonderful people exposed the templates and frameworks that had previously positioned the gospel as a formula in my mind: 'Behave, think, or feel in a certain way, and you will be blessed. Don't behave, think, or feel in this way and you have no promise.'

Through many private exchanges, my previous template of expectations was quickly dismantled and thrown out. The diversity of faith and perspective was vast.

I completely loved the members of my ward and wanted to do everything I could to help them find God and to feel safe at church. And so I started to read and research. I wanted to understand. I wanted to be able to empathise. I wanted to be able to help in any way that I could. In my efforts to help them, I began to struggle in my own faith. There was no map to follow and I could see that it wouldn't do for a bishop to admit he too was struggling. So I kept things to myself. Very soon I began to feel alone. At 24, I knew that I loved Jesus Christ but as I began to challenge some of the things I felt I knew, I struggled to find peace. My studies led to more questions and concerns and all while sitting at the front, in full view of my ward.

In hindsight, I can clearly see how my faith was maturing – moving from a dependence on the Church to a dependence on Christ. Mindsets that had sustained me in previous years were no longer sufficient to carry me forward. I never felt I was in a crisis of faith, back then I didn't have that vocabulary, but I did have to work very hard to reposition what I based my faith on.

I found it hard to balance my work as a financial services analyst with a gruelling weekly schedule and workload, my calling as bishop, and life as a newly-wed. Only sometimes did I feel like my prayers were heard. As I served my ward members, I continued to be exposed to their concerns and challenges. I began to fatigue and to feel uncomfortable serving as the bishop. I often thought, how can I support all these people and meet their expectations of me? How can I respond to their questions when I have my own? How can I help them find peace, when I am struggling for peace in my own life?

Perhaps in an effort to self-medicate, I tried to focus the ward on the Saviour and His healing power. I became less interested in a high-performance Christ and much more reliant on the healing Christ. As I established stronger personal connection with Him, I felt strength return to my soul and to my service. But it wasn't at the flick of a switch. It took time. It was a journey characterised by moments of light and periods of wandering alone. Looking back, from a place of strength and deeper conversion today, I see how kind and merciful the Lord was to me. I see how He blessed my family and helped both Jen and me advance in our faith journeys. My own experiences undoubtedly shaped my service and how I tried to turn people to Christ's mercy and love.

At that time, as a bishopric, we tried to help everybody in the ward enjoy three things: 1) connection to the Saviour, 2) spiritual safety through a good Sunday experience, and 3) activities that brought us together in unity. In those spaces, I found joy and motivation. As my focus on Him grew and grew, I felt my heavy heart begin to heal. He restored and strengthened my faith in Him.

We encouraged our members to start from where they were at, in their seeking connection with Jesus Christ. We recommended them for the temple when they were struggling and striving. We agreed that if people's personal interpretations looked different to those of others, that was okay. We focused on helping them to progress, growing in light and truth along their own path to Jesus Christ. We trusted that He would lead them, teach them, and sanctify them, that through their personal growth they would make choices and changes that would lead them to happiness and joy. Almost twenty years ago, we put no arbitrary hurdles in front of people and we didn't hold up the temple recommend as the day-one standard. We loved people and invited them to connect to Him, on His timetable and on their timetable. Throughout these years, I felt like I was the primary beneficiary of the culture we created. Although we didn't use these words, we embraced a Come as You Are mindset and created a culture where all could feel that they belonged.

Before long, labels like 'unorthodox' and 'liberal' started to attach themselves to our approach. Sometimes it was a compliment that created space for others. At other times it was a criticism. When our daughter was born, we moved out of London. Leaving the ward was a real wrench.

Four years later, I was called to serve in the stake presidency. We had just turned thirty and we were expecting our third child. We were given time and space to consider the invitation to serve and Jen and I both felt the spirit of the call. We accepted. Five years later, our stake president was released, a new president was called, and I was called back into the new stake presidency, offering some continuity to the new leadership team. Nearly nine years on the stake presidency again had a profound effect upon my faith.

During my years of service on the stake presidency, I again spent time with struggling members of the church. Many of the challenges were the same from when I served as bishop, but now they were more amplified by the internet. Struggling members were now much more exposed to alternative narratives and histories to those the Church had always taught. Again, people had questions and they were becoming more adept at finding, and relying upon, online opinions. Their frustrations with their own church experience were now more easily linked to similar experiences elsewhere around the world. As an observer, I again felt that a great feeling of loss was impacting their spiritual lives. It all happened so fast that many local, lay leaders were neither ready, nor equipped, to deal with the rip-saw effect. Similar to my own experience, faithful leaders were finding things out for the first time themselves, as struggling souls shared in confidence what they were learning online.

This time, I observed the Church moving quickly to write and release online Gospel Topics Essays covering subjects where people felt the prevailing cultural and historical narratives were at best incomplete and at worst like information had been hidden. Seminary and Institute curricula were updated to include broader perspectives. Digital content more ably supported local teachers to improve local engagement. Professors of religion, talented authors, and the podcast community helped many find a path to faith. Today we appear to be much better equipped in this space, but the collateral damage to that portion of the rising generation—the millennials—was dramatic.

Many friends left the Church within a seven-year period. Each had their own reasons which broadly fell into three groups: some undertook, in their own words, 'obsessive investigations' of the Church's truth claims and were left unconvinced. Some became offended by local leaders and couldn't reconcile them behaving in such a way and being 'called by God' (or having to sustain them as a requirement to access temple blessings). Others left because they felt their own values weren't reflected in the cultures or teachings of the Church.

It wasn't only my friends. As a member of the stake presidency, most of my one-to-ones with people, most often in temple recommend interviews, was them sharing the anguish of their faith deconstruction. They couldn't find Christ at church—and if He was there, he was buried under too many layers of sediment.

Perhaps because of my experiences as a bishop, none of what people were calling new information felt new to me. I had transitioned my faith to Christ and was able to see the challenges as catalysts to necessary, albeit painful, faith reconstructions. I felt I had a handle on the arguments and complaints and could articulate thoughtful challenges and even empathetic, constructive agreement, always pointing them to Him. I didn't shut people down. I gave them space and heard them out. I wasn't professionally trained, but I knew how to help somebody feel heard and reassured. I tried to pivot them to faith in God, a relationship with Jesus Christ, and the role an imperfect church experience can play in His divine plan. We talked about a continuing restoration and the role of the living prophet. Perhaps because of the approach, or maybe just because I was in the stake presidency, most of my time was spent in this space. I gave many blessings during these years and always felt the love God had for these wonderful people. These were not antagonists fighting against the Church. These were people hurt and confused by what might be called church-trauma.

In discussion with my wife, my parents, and my mentors, I devised a model, a mindset shift that has given my faith in Christ more space. I called my model 'Splitting My Circles.'

As I have shared this model, many have found space for their faith in Christ, their place in the covenant, and a loyalty to the long term aims and ambitions of the Church. Just as looking for Christ's healing nature in the scriptures requires time, effort, and diligence, searching for His healing and restorative nature in our local church experience can require patience, faith, and personal revelation.

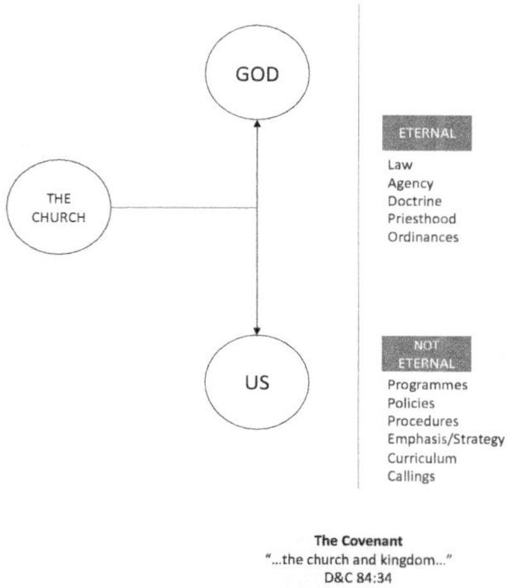

Figure 3

Like all models and frameworks, Figure 3 is a simplification. It has two sides, the left-hand side and the right-hand side, and proposes that there are two ways to view the relationship between "the church and kingdom."[119]

Common to both the left and right-hand side is the premise that our connection, through Christ, to our loving God is central to our faith and that the new and everlasting covenant is how He invites us to progress and return to Him. Where the two sides of the dichotomy differ is how each side approaches the role of the Church in supporting this divine connection and covenant relationship.

119 Doctrine and Covenants 84:34

Looking at the left-hand side first, it has been my experience that many of our young people start their faith journey supported by a single circle. Their connection to God is found at church, informed by church, and defined by church. Whether it be through Primary, Youth lessons, Seminary and Institute, the mission field, and into young adulthood, for many, their relationship with the Church is their faith experience. For them, the one-circle approach works well. The Church of Jesus Christ of Latter-day Saints is the kingdom of God. By joining the Church, people make and enter into a covenant relationship with Christ. At church, they find the gospel of Jesus Christ, teachings about His Atonement and Resurrection and access to His priesthood ordinances. In the Church, living prophets speak God's mind and will to help us understand His doctrine. Through the Church, God reveals and implements His divine policies and procedures to govern His people within the covenant. Where there is complexity, difficulty, ambiguity, or where there is pain, it is the members that must learn, mature, and change.

On the right-hand side of the framework, connection to God again remains the focus. He invites us to come unto Him through His covenant. Those who choose Him and enter into the covenant become His covenant people. However, on the right-hand side, what was one circle supporting our covenant relationship with God has now been *split* into two circles, one to represent the kingdom of God and one to represent The Church of Jesus Christ of Latter-day Saints. Here the focus and priority is again placed on our connection to, and covenant relationship with, God, through the Son. Everything in the kingdom of God is eternal. It will be with us in the next life and existed before this life. Here we live by eternal law and unchanging doctrine while experiencing the prioritisation of agency, justice and mercy, ordinances, priesthood, and all the principles of the gospel of Jesus Christ, as taught by living prophets. Even the most unhappy and disaffected commentator would have to agree that if there were a perfect way to experience a covenant relationship with a loving and nurturing God, through eternal and entirely affirming means, it would bring joy and happiness to their lives and would be hard to vote against.

The right-hand side also recognises that today, in its current form, The Church of Jesus Christ of Latter-day Saints is not yet Zion complete. It is not yet the promised land and has not yet been fully restored into what the covenant community will one day become. The right-hand side diagram recognises that God continues to build the Church into His kingdom, but that His perfect kingdom exists separate from the Church today. Both are important to establish and strengthen our covenant connection to Him, but the Church has human frailties within it that the kingdom of God does not. Someday the Church will become the kingdom of God, but today it exists in an enabling and separate circle.

Suggesting that the Church is a perfect space to somebody who more comfortably identifies with the right-hand side is a tough place to start a discussion about faith in Jesus Christ. For them, much of the scaffolding in the Church circle is eventually temporary. In other words, it will continue to experience change, with certain elements (including programmes, policies, and procedures) being replaced as the continuing Restoration unfolds and the promised destiny of the Church and kingdom of God is fulfilled.

For those preferring the right-hand side, the Church is 'The kingdom of God on the earth,' a vehicle to help gather people into the actual kingdom of God via His covenant on both sides of the veil. For them The Church of Jesus Christ of Latter-day Saints is a custodian of priesthood keys and a delivery system for the Atonement of Jesus Christ through the provision of priesthood ordinances. It is also their local faith community and the place they learn the doctrine of Christ. For those on the right-hand side, it isn't—and doesn't need to be a—perfect local experience. For them, both circles are within the covenant. In fact, they make and join the covenant through the enabling church circle. By splitting the one circle into two circles, they create more space for their faith. They appreciate the difference between their personal faith in Christ and the structures which exist to support that faith.

Now importantly, not everybody needs to split the circles into two. And that is perfectly fine. Some are completely satisfied with the left-hand side. For them, the gospel and the Church circles are one, or at least overlap almost entirely. Their connection to God and the Church is a safe place that defines their spirituality, teaches them doctrine, and provides them with priesthood ordinances. They don't have as many questions. They don't think about it too much. They don't understand why others have so many questions, and they live their faith in relative comfort. They don't see as much ambiguity or complexity. Their spiritual life feels relatively simple and straightforward. For them, it's enough that the fulness of the gospel is taught in The Church of Jesus Christ of Latter-day Saints. For them, its policies and programmes are designed by God and issued directly through His appointed leaders. Although they have empathy for those who struggle and want to do whatever they can to support them, they just don't see it the same way. No doubt, there are lots of young people like this in the Church.

There are others however who really struggle with the left-hand side. For them, the complexity and ambiguity can at times be difficult to bear. They may ask how a church that claims to not only follow Christ but to actually be led by Him can have "made mistakes," to quote President Uchtdorf.[120] They may struggle with the notion that prophets are infallible. Moreover, given the teachings of some historical prophets in former paradigms, at different points along the timeline of the continuing restoration, they may struggle to switch off an internal voice that tells them that today's living prophets are tomorrow's historical prophets.

Those who favour the right-hand side might struggle with existing church cultures that they feel exclude people or contrast with their own personal values. They may hold on to the idea that similar teachings from former paradigms were proven to be at best temporary and at worst unlikely to have come from God. For these and many other personal reasons, for some, believing that the Church is the literal kingdom of God is currently a stumbling block. They intuitively understand the counsel from Elder Neal A. Maxwell then of the Presidency of the Seventy in 1980:

120 Dieter F. Uchtdorf, *Come, Join with Us*, General Conference (Salt Lake City: The Church of Jesus Christ of Latter-day Saints, October 2013), Gospel Library App.

> He [or she] understands the difference between ends and means and sees that some Church aids are, in a sense, scaffolding for the soul, which scaffolding one day will be removed—like waterwings or training wheels.[121]

Elder Maxwell, newly called to the Quorum of the Twelve Apostles, would go on to say in general conference, two years later:

> In our striving to be prepared, therefore, let us be careful to rely on parents, priesthood, and principles—and on scriptures, and temples, and leaders who lead—to see us through. Let us not mistake program scaffolding for substance.[122]

For this group, the right-hand side diagram can be a way to create more space to grow faith in Jesus Christ. In our efforts to support our young people with a church experience that focuses on Jesus Christ as presented by the Lord's living prophet, consider these three excerpts from perspectives of faithful, local Church leaders. Each of them identifies as somebody who recognises the differences between the kingdom of God and the vehicle of the Church.

Wrote one:

> I consider myself a convert in the Church but not a convert to the Church. My conversion—and my faith—centres on Jesus Christ. I value my membership enormously, in so far as it enables me to join the covenant and gives me a community. I also have a strong personal testimony that we are led by the Lord's prophet in the Church. I need the Church. It has done so much for me. Nobody can live the gospel in a vacuum. Nobody can strive to alleviate suffering the way Christ did, sitting alone in their house. I'm grateful for the Church and what it has helped me to prioritise, and how it continues to teach me. Admit-

121 Neil A. Maxwell, *True Believers in Christ*, BYU Devotional, Oct 7th, 1980. https://speeches.byu.edu/talks/neal-a-maxwell/true-believers-christ/#:~:text=Let%20us%2C%20brothers%20and%20sisters,assigned%20gatekeeper%20is%20Jesus%20Christ.

122 Neal A. Maxwell, *Be of Good Cheer,* General Conference (Salt Lake City: The Church of Jesus Christ of Latter-day Saints, October 1982), Gospel Library App.

tedly, there are parts of my church experience that are more challenging, in ways that I don't expect the kingdom of God to be. The focus of my own volunteer ministry has been to stay close to the prophet, to strive to personally live the two great commandments, and to connect as many people as possible to Christ. I try and observe what our local needs are and do my best to help people feel that they belong.[123]

Wrote another:

I really enjoy my faith in Jesus Christ and feel close to Him. I'm happiest when I feel it defining me. I also accept that I need to go to church and I'm happy to do what I'm asked to do. But I don't let my church experience define me. The Church is a complex organisation trying to create the right balance between global uniformity and local freedoms. I've spent a lot of time being frustrated by things that could be done so much better, in my opinion. But more often than not, I've also benefited from greater perspective by realising that what works for me doesn't always work for them. These connections always help my determination to be more humble and teachable. I've also learned to see only good intentions behind the complexity. The Church is learning how to innovate top-down as well as bottom-up and it wouldn't serve anybody if it tipped over into chaos. The Lord won't let that happen. It's not easy but I feel like I am empowered enough to make the necessary changes in my own sphere of influence, in how members experience the Church. I really value that.[124]

And finally:

Christ is my focus. As the Church inevitably grows more accustomed to diversity and works harder to deliver a more representative global leadership team—whether that be defined by gender, race, or nationality—I believe there are lots of reasons to be optimistic. It took me a long time to realise that a lot of what I experience in the Church is coming from committees of people in Utah who are trying hard to better understand my life and my needs. I've made peace with it. Relatedly, I am particularly excited by the growing influence and impact the rising generation will have on the Church. They will push and pull

123 Personal Correspondence

124 Personal Correspondence

> our culture into new spaces of inclusion and representation. If we follow the prophet and listen to our young people, the inevitable cycles of prophetic redesign will enable us to help many more people – just as the Church has been divinely established to do.[125]

The purpose of the above, circle-splitting framework is not to introduce new language or to gild the lily with yet another layer. The purpose of the framework is to simply point our young people to greater, and more prioritised, connection to God and His kingdom. Through this framework, not only can our young people who struggle with their church experience, learn to understand its purpose, see the bigger picture, and continue to come unto Christ, but their generational cohort can find the mindset to be part of its continuing restoration. They will be able to balance being patient with speaking up and being part of the change they want to see.

All this said, the right-hand side comes with a warning, one that is especially important for the rising generation. The purpose of the model is not to diminish or relegate the importance of our membership in the Church or to disrespect or minimise the prophets and general leaders called to be witnesses of Christ, teach divine doctrines, receive revelation, and make strategic and tactical organisational decisions on our behalf. This is important.

If the rising generation convince themselves that the Church is irrelevant, or deserves to be dismissed or relegated, they've tragically missed the point.

Elder Uchtdorf taught:

> [Truth] is contained in the gospel of Jesus Christ. And the fulness of that gospel is taught in The Church of Jesus Christ of Latter-day Saints. Jesus Christ said, "I am the way, the truth, and the life: no man cometh unto the Father, but by me."[126]

125 Personal Correspondence

126 Dieter F. Uchtdorf, *Jesus Christ Is the Strength of Youth*, General Conference (Salt Lake City: The Church of Jesus Christ of Latter-day Saints, October 2022), Gospel Library App.

Our young people need the gospel and the Church to help them find abiding connection with God. Rejecting their membership in the Church as unimportant will not lead to the rest that Christ promises.

At FSY, Jen and I shared with our youth and young adults that we hold our membership in the Church in high regard. But we don't consider ourselves disciples of *the Church.* We are members of the Church and aspire to be disciples of *Jesus Christ,* learning His doctrine, following the principles of His gospel and finding our path within our local community. We attend because here we find joy in the covenant. Here we find the Lord's prophet. Here we find access to priesthood keys and ordinances—including the sacrament, and in the temple—for ourselves and our family. We attend so that we can worship God through prayer, music, and personal repentance. We attend so that we can draw strength from the love and camaraderie of the place in which we are planted, hoping to contribute in a similar way. We value the physical environment that allows us the opportunity to mourn with those that mourn, comfort those who stand in need of comfort and bear one another's burdens.[127] In turn, we value the blessing of having friends who do the same for us. We choose to serve in our community through our callings, and we have experienced great personal growth in this way. In turn, our family has been blessed by the service of others doing the same. Finally, we attend so that we can feel close to our loving Heavenly Father, devote ourselves to our Saviour Jesus Christ, and receive revelation through the Holy Ghost. But we don't ever expect the local space to be perfect – and yes, sometimes it is frustrating. We recognise that we too are part of the culture that impacts upon others' experiences – for good and bad!

When our young people get frustrated, when our culture and traditions create pain and distractions, or when local leadership appears to lessen their experience, I would hope that they remember these words from Eugene England:

> In the life of the true Church, there are constant opportunities for all to serve, especially to learn to serve people we would not normally choose to serve—or possibly even associate with—and thus opportunities to

127 Mosiah 18:9

> learn to love unconditionally. There is constant encouragement, even pressure, to be "active": to "have a calling" and thus to have to grapple with relationships and management, with other people's ideas and wishes, their feelings and failures; to attend classes and meetings and to have to listen to other people's sometimes misinformed or prejudiced notions and to have to make some constructive response; to have leaders and occasionally to be hurt by their weakness and blindness, even unrighteous dominion; and then to be made a leader and find that you, too, with all the best intentions, can be weak and blind and unrighteous. Church involvement teaches us compassion and patience as well as courage and discipline. It makes us responsible for the personal and marital, physical, and spiritual welfare of people we may not already love (or may even heartily dislike), and thus we learn to love them. It stretches and challenges us, though disappointed and exasperated, in ways we would not otherwise choose to be—and thus gives us a chance to be made better than we might choose to be, but ultimately need and want to be.[128]

The proposed framework isn't about picking one circle over the other, and it isn't about elevating one and relegating the other. As leaders, teachers, and parents, we can teach the rising generation that we need both circles. By splitting them, however, there may be more space for connection, understanding, generosity, and faith in Jesus Christ.

By celebrating people for coming as they are, inviting them to connect with Him unto healing, and shifting our teachings and vocabulary to be more inclusive, we will help others become more confident in *their* faith, as well as *the* faith. We will encourage the rising generation to continue growing in their faith and others to come back to their faith. I believe we will all feel more sanctified by His Spirit as we work with those holding priesthood keys to increase the feeling of belonging in our wards and stakes. I believe we can build a faith community we can all feel proud to be a part of.

---

128 Eugene England, "Why the Church Is As True As the Gospel," *Sunstone* 22, nos. 3/4 (June 1999), 61–69. https://www.eugeneengland.org/why-the-church-is-as-true-as-the-gospel

Chapter Summary

Our young people appear to have a more analytical and pragmatic approach towards the Church as an organisation, compared with that of their parents and grandparents.

It is important for the rising generation to understand the difference between the Church and the kingdom of God and how the two interact as they prepare to make and keep covenants with God.

Creating Space for the Diversity of Faith

My faith is important to me, but I am really private about it. I often feel bad, as I know I'm expected to be a better member missionary. I don't want my friends to think I'm being preachy or for them to judge me. It also bothers me that I have so many questions. Most of my church friends don't seem to have any.

Adam, 17

JEN AND I WERE CALLED BACK TO FSY LONDON FOR A SECOND YEAR which gave our team a chance to build on the message of inclusion and belonging along with other successes we had with Come as You Are. During the second year, our focus was on helping the rising generation feel proud of the faith they have. As such, *#proudofmyfaith* featured in the lesson content during the following year's summer programme. These two connected messages, #comeasyouare and #proudofmyfaith, served as reassurances to the youth and young adults that their journeys to Christ can be filled with a quiet confidence that fully validated their starting points and their circumstances. The messages helped remind the youth and young adults that their faith can grow with time and with new experiences. Helping them to understand that they didn't have to get it all right immediately enabled them to feel drawn, not pushed, towards His healing power.

For the rising generation, figuring out who they are and what path they should take can be difficult. Many appear to feel the responsibility of representing *the* faith before they feel supported or sustained by their *personal* faith.

Although many young people are able to travel admirably in what appear to be relatively straight lines, others struggle. When those who struggle feel that their faith isn't enough, that their faith is different than others, or that it doesn't match the faith demonstrated in lessons, stories, and talks, they can feel alone at church and be put off by the idea that they don't belong. When our youth and young adults feel this way, the 'all-in' or 'all-out' delusions causes too many to turn away. For some, feeling pressed to share their faith before they feel sustained by it can make church harder.

Even when our young people come as they are and feel more connected to Him, they may still feel awkward amongst their friends who don't share their faith. In the good times, being different can be empowering and emboldening; in the bad times, being different can be lonely and discouraging. Although the answer may well be to get involved, to step into the dark, and to exercise some faith, many would benefit from greater levels of empathy and reassurance before they're willing to take responsibility.

Consider these two perspectives on missionary work shared by a young woman and a young man:

> How am I supposed to share the gospel with my friends? I'm not sure where to start. I don't know anything. My older sister has got so much faith, my younger sister too. In our family, I get left behind. I'm the lost sheep of the family. We even joke about it. I'm just different. When my friends ask me what I believe, I usually just change the subject. Then I feel even worse.

> Sometimes, I feel like the gospel is for good people who, like a car, just need to fine-tune themselves or dust themselves off. But what happens when your car isn't just a bit dusty? What happens when it has only

> got one wheel and an exhaust hanging off? Although I know I need to be better and want to do the right things, the reality is that I've done and said things I can't undo. My teammates know about all of it. If I'm honest, I live a bit of a double life. I'm not a bad person, I jut find it hard to be the same person at church and at school. There is no way I can share the gospel with them. First, they would laugh at me, and then, if I kept pushing, they'd call me a hypocrite.

Feelings like these are common to many of our young people. Bringing more authenticity into our church environment would lessen the pressure our young people can feel to be one person at school and another person at church. Feeling like they can be themselves in both environments, no matter what, would surely reduce some of the cognitive dissonance they can feel when learning the gospel at church. Of course, the ability to do this is influenced by a number of factors – not least by how closely aligned their school cultures are with their church cultures.

As an example, life in the UK is not like Utah or other Midwestern cultures in the US where the faith tradition is the dominant culture. Despite our shared English language, the Church in the UK has its own unique identity. This impacts the way the gospel is experienced.

Many summers ago, we visited friends in Utah. One evening, whilst we were out on the driveway talking, we noticed three men walking down the middle of the quiet, suburban road. They were dressed in white shirts and ties but looked too old to be full-time missionaries and weren't wearing name badges. "Who are those guys?" I asked. "Oh, that's our bishopric," said our host. "On Wednesday nights they hold their bishopric meeting. In the warmer weather, they prefer to meet out in the community to get some exercise and to see who in the ward might need support. Our ward is basically these six streets, so it works out really well." I was stunned. It helped me appreciate how different my church experiences were and why I was sometimes harder on myself than I needed to be. I thought about the nights I tried to do three home teaching visits in one evening but couldn't get across town through the traffic and had to cancel the third appointment. I thought about the regular 50-minute, one-way drives to the stake centre for a heavy, weekly schedule of church meetings, trainings, and conferences.

For our young people here in the UK, active religion is not the norm. There is limited Christian air-cover in our society. Their neighbours aren't members of the Church and the chapel isn't two streets over. Here they are most often the only member of the Church in their school, university, and place of work. Moreover, they are most likely the only Latter-day Saint their friends have ever met or even heard of.

Whilst some might rejoice in the opportunity to be a pioneer, for many, standing alone can make faith feel fragile. Not everybody is equipped to be a pathfinder. And those who are can't do it all the time. Being reminded regularly to do more, either within the faith or with those not of the faith, while being benchmarked to a culture that is not your own creates fatigue.

Growing up inside the Church, there were also not-so-subtle tells that I lived a foreign faith. Lesson manuals referred to anecdotes with dollars, mountain trails, canyons, snowy winters, fast offering collections by the deacons, seminary classes inside school buildings, shortening (I still don't know what shortening is!), and the protagonists of the anecdotal stories were named Chad, Todd, and Chrissy (names added for effect). These anecdotes would be shared in Church meetings and youth lessons, as though they were completely normal.

Standing to recite in unison, or chant the Young Women's theme or (more recently) the Young Men's theme in a British chapel—whilst completely normal to children in Utah who stand to pledge allegiance to the flag from an early age in the school classroom—is just not something the Brits did, or have done since, in any other environment. It is not a British thing to do and so feels uncomfortable and inauthentic for many of the young women and young men.

Although the intense Americana of the faith was attractive inside the safety of the bubble where I rather enjoyed the roadshows, Gold and Green Balls, a basketball hoop in the chapel, a water fountain, and family holidays to Utah, outside of the faith community, I often felt like I had something to hide. Being reminded in seminary that I should not be "ashamed of the gospel of Jesus Christ,"[129] didn't help. Feeling proud of my faith was a fleeting and fragile feeling.

In the UK, missionary invitations were also a source of insecurity. Our congregations might be only a hundred members at most, with the average stake size measured in the hundreds not the thousands. As such, each ward typically has at least one pair of missionaries and sometimes more.

Although I loved the missionaries growing up and still look forward to their visits today, as Brits, our family had a lot of exposure resulting from missionary invitations and the expectations that followed. When your pool of friends doesn't change that much (if at all) from one year to another, such expectations become burdensome, especially when you are trying to figure out if faith in Christ is for you.

However, challenges aside, building a refreshing, revitalising, and sustaining faith in the Lord Jesus Christ is joyful, enriching, and even life-changing. Partaking of the fruit of the gospel of Jesus Christ brings joy and lasting happiness. Connection with God is anything but awkward and burdensome.

Said a wise young friend:

> I'm happiest when I live the gospel. I've made some mistakes and even some big ones. But I know the difference between fake happiness and real joy. My church friends have become some of my best friends. I look forward to stake events and multi-stake activities. The youth are such a strength to me. I love getting together in large groups. It really helps me know that this is a place that I can come to and feel safe. I know I've got a lot to learn, but I can see what the gospel does for people's lives. I hope it will do the same for mine. I know I could probably share it more with people, but right now, I just love being part of it. I'll get to that bit later, when I'm ready. With time, I could totally see myself inviting my best friends at school into this space. It will be a natural next step, I guess.[130]

Thinking through how we can create spaces for the rising generation to discover how they can each feel supported and sustained by

129 Romans 1:16

130 Personal Correspondence

their personal faith should be a priority for local leaders. Invitations to share their faith with others should never overwhelm the youth. If they feel loved and supported by their faith, they will naturally want to share it with their friends.

In his letter to the Saints in Ephesus, Paul teaches us how to think about our faith to help us bond with it and feel proud of it. Feeling proud of our faith is a function of feeling sustained by and connected to it. He likened following Jesus Christ to putting on a suit of armour. He wrote,

> Wherefore take unto you the whole armour of God, that ye may be able to withstand in the evil day, and having done all, to stand. . . . Above all, taking the *shield of faith*, wherewith ye shall be able to quench all the fiery darts of the wicked.[131]

It is notable that Paul chose the shield to represent faith in Jesus Christ, not the sword. It makes sense that faith in Christ would be positioned as defensive and protective, able to parry, deflect, or (to use Paul's word) 'quench' the adversary's projectiles. It makes sense that he positioned faith as something we can, when necessary, hide and crouch behind, saving us from danger, limiting our pain and enabling us to wait out difficult times.

Finding their voices and their courage to "stand as a witness"[132] will come in time. If we as their leaders, teachers, and parents spend more time helping our young people to feel sustained by their faith in Christ, not only will they invite their friends, but they'll do it in their own authentic ways. But even without the thought of increasing member-missionary work, the desirable end goal is for them to feel safe and protected by their faith. If their shield is being asked to function in a capacity that isn't sustaining and safe for them, they are less likely to find it enriching and worthwhile in the long run.

For the rising generation, it might be that by refocusing their faith in Jesus Christ as a shield they will find more authenticity, more confidence, and more spiritual and psychological safety. Too much sword

---

131 Ephesians 6:13, 16 emphasis added

132 Mosiah 18:9

and not enough shield may well be a recipe for difficulty in the long run.

For those who can relate, too much sword, or weaponised faith, pushes natural conversations with friends into inauthentic exchanges. Inauthenticity is an enemy to blossoming faith. It takes general and sincere enquiries and responds to them with recruitment strategies. This is something to which the rising generation is deeply averse to.

To help strengthen their shield and create faith they can feel proud of, we should encourage the rising generation to be their authentic selves with their friends with healthy friendships as the end-goal. We want them to build lasting friendships that support them and help them feel that they belong. As those friendships that were built on authenticity and trust grow into personal networks, faith in God will become a natural extension of who they are. If and when they feel prompted and courageous enough to be more open, they will feel comfortable in the safety of their friendship. Removing the pressure, the push, the sale, or the agenda is an important change to make so that they feel proud of the faith they have.

As their leaders, teachers, and parents, we need to encourage them to find a more personal approach to the discussion in a way that sustains and normalises their faith. I know from my own experiences what it's like to be caught off-guard by questions that I didn't know how to answer. Even as a returned-missionary, I've found myself at parties, work events, in bars, and restaurants, with people asking for the doctrinal differences compared to other Christian denominations which in turn have led my sharing Joseph Smith's First Vision when it probably wasn't the right moment to do so.

Recently, when asked about a documentary on the Church, I was asked by close friends not of our faith if I felt that the programme was a reflection of who we are as a people and what we believe as a family. The documentary was unflattering in parts and had amplified a number of myths, shining an uncomfortable light on practices that created an editorial edge and sensationalism. Sadly, they weren't all untrue or out of date. One friend asked: "You're not like that, so when I watched it, I assumed it couldn't possibly be true. What did you think of the programme?"

Rather than talk about my Church, I split my circles and spoke about my faith in Jesus Christ. I didn't weaponise the discussion. I didn't testify, and I didn't attempt to recruit my friend. I simply spoke about my shield. I spoke about why I tried to follow Jesus Christ and why I loved His teachings about inclusion, kindness, and love. I shared that because I worship Him, it made it easier when I found my faith tradition more challenging. Because of my shield (and not my sword), my friends were empathetic and warm. They shared their own perspectives and experiences at their own church communities growing up. The discussion ended very positively. We all felt included and safe within our trusted spaces. The simple description of my shield of faith —as opposed to the wielding of my weapons of faith—delivered an authentic exchange which created more space for my own faith journey to Jesus Christ.

We can teach the rising generation to take similar approaches in their own discussions with their friends. Some ideas of how to discuss the shield of faith might include the following. They aren't meant to be scripts but hopefully tonal shifts from the sword to the shield is clear:

(1) "Yes, I am religious. I'm a Christian and I believe in Jesus Christ. It's something my family taught me, but I have to say I love it. My faith gives me a real sense of purpose and helps me cope when life gets hard."

(2) "Not for me, thank you. I don't drink. Why? My faith is really important to me, and I try and stay away from that sort of thing. I don't judge anybody, but, for me, this is a code I'm trying to live by."

(3) "I guess my faith is my diversity. It's what makes me different, also it's what makes me strong. I think it's great that we celebrate people's diversity so much today. It gives me courage to accept how I am different, the value this can bring to me and to my friendships without feeling judged."

Feeling proud of their faith will become easier for our young people when they learn to talk about it in ways that strengthen them, as opposed to ways that push it onto others. Contrived invitations or inauthentic exchanges shouldn't ever be part of sharing their faith.

Regarding member missionary work, we can all accept that the Lord is gathering His people – perhaps focusing first on those who recognise and respond to His voice. When we are baptised, we take his name upon us His name and covenant to stand as a witness of Him. With their shield in place, as our young people feel prompted and in a way that will feel completely natural, they will be amazed to find the confidence that comes from speaking about their cherished faith with their friends. But we don't have to teach them to force it or feel like they are expected to force it, especially before they have found it.

I know from my own experiences that people are respectful and more often than not accept sincere invitations to come to Church, a baptismal service, or a church activity. They always feel grateful for generous invitations over something of such personal importance. But no push and no selling. No sword. No weapon. The Lord will hasten His work with the friends of the rising generation. Their friends are His children too.

With their shield in place, our young people will do incredible things. They will be better prepared for their life-long journeys of faith as they love and feel sustained by the spaces they occupy.

Another way we can support their faith in Christ and their desire to come unto Him is by reassuring them that its okay if their faith looks different from that of other people! Like Lehi's vision of the tree of life, although there is just one tree, everybody makes their own journey to it. We can all make more space for the diversity of faith and one way to do this is to value the different ways our young people seek and process truth. Although some may not have many questions, others seem to have nothing but questions. There needs to be space for both approaches by remembering and teaching that both have value.

Regarding the story of Lehi's vision in the Book of Mormon, Rosalynde Frandsen Welch observed an interesting difference between Lehi and Nephi's approach to faith. Building out her original insight from Lehi's initial description of the vision, she notes that Lehi never asks any questions.[133]

Lehi's vision begins with him being in a dark and dreary wilderness. Without asking how he got there, he simply records that he is met by a man who tells him to follow him. And so he does. He doesn't know who the man is, where he comes from or where they are headed. He just follows him.

After hours without apparently getting anywhere, Lehi begins to pray. In his prayer, instead of asking for directions, an estimated time of arrival, or even an idea as to the destination, he simply asks for mercy.

Then he sees the spacious field and the tree. Again, he doesn't ask anything, he just walks over to the tree and starts eating its fruit. Nobody tells him to, and he doesn't ask what type of fruit it is, whether it is in season, how it grows, or whether he needs permission to eat it. All he knows is that it makes him happy.

Still, without any questions, he knows that his family will enjoy it too, so he calls them over. In his vision, he mentions some other things – a river, an iron rod, a mist of darkness, a great building – but he doesn't explain any of it. His focus is on the tree. He is happy to be enjoying the fruit and sad that not all his family wanted to do the same.

Now, the rising generation have questions about many aspects of their lives. However, when it comes to matters of faith, many of them are like Lehi. They just don't have many questions. Lehi is a faith-filled man for whom the exquisiteness of tasting God's mercy and love outweighs the need for explanation. Like him, many of our young people enjoy what the gospel offers, the simplicity of eating the fruit and tasting of God's overwhelming love. They may not need to puzzle over every aspect of what it means. Perhaps like those who favour the left-hand side in the previous chapter, for them, the only explanation needed is found in Isaiah:

133 Rosalynde Welch, "How to Do Things with Doubt," *Journal of Book of Mormon Studies*. Vol. 28: No. 1, Article 10. BYU Neal A, Maxwell Institute for Religious Scholarship, 2019. https://scholarsarchive.byu.edu/jbms/vol28/iss1/10

> For my thoughts are not your thoughts, neither are your ways my ways, saith the Lord. For as the heavens are higher than the earth, so are my ways higher than your ways and my thoughts than your thoughts.[134]

For them, God has all the answers, and that's enough. Such believers know the fruit makes them happy, and they simply want to enjoy it with their loved ones. If it has a deeper meaning, they'll learn what they need as they go along. Yes, many of the rising generation are like Lehi.

So, if Lehi's account doesn't pose questions or explain his vision, how do we know so much about its meaning? Simply put, it's because Nephi asks lots of questions.

When the Spirit visits Nephi and asks him what he wants, Nephi says he wants to see what his father saw.[135] The Spirit asks: "Do you believe what your father saw?" Nephi replies: "Yea, thou knowest that I believe all the words of my father."

Nephi is a faith-filled man too. If asked what quality we most associate with Nephi, most of us might say faith unto action. But for Nephi, simply believing someone else's words or trusting someone else's experience isn't enough on this occasion. When he is shown the tree, Nephi acknowledges it as "precious above all." But when he is asked what he wants, he doesn't ask to taste it there and then. He asks "to know the interpretation thereof." Doubtless, he experiences the love of God many other times, but right then he wants to understand. There are also many of the rising generation like Nephi.

We should teach the lessons of this comparison to our young people.

Having faith in God, even great faith, is NOT incompatible with having questions, and lots of them. It's not wrong to wonder about parts of the gospel or the Church. The key is to encourage them to ask their questions with an open sincere heart that can cope without immediate answers or absolute certainty Answers come very differently to a closed, cynical heart that demands clear answers quickly.

---

134 Isaiah 55:8-9

135 1 Nephi 11

Of course, no one is completely like Lehi (asking absolutely no questions) or completely like Nephi (needing lots of explanations). It is the case that some want to question the meaning of things more than others, and they feel frustrated when they're not explained to their satisfaction.

It also suggests there are two ways to achieve spiritual understanding, Lehi's 'tasting' or 'experiencing' and Nephi's 'searching' or 'investigating.' They're both valid and not mutually exclusive. The rising generation might lean towards one more than the other, which leads us to another conclusion. Whether they are a 'Lehi' or a 'Nephi,' we need to make room for both types in the Church. The Church of Jesus Christ is 'home' for both types of faith and lots of other different kinds of faith too. And we can help every one of our young people feel proud of the faith they have.

Those who want some aspects of the gospel or the Church clarified shouldn't look upon those who don't as though their faith is 'blind' and therefore less authentic, less valid, less tested. To them, tasting the fruit is enough, especially when it has come at great personal cost; the exquisiteness of knowing the love of God is enough. How can it not be enough?

"And this is life eternal, that they might know thee the only true God, and Jesus Christ, whom thou hast sent."[136]

Equally those who are content to experience the gospel fruit without knowing how it grew shouldn't look upon those with questions as being troubled, troublesome, as having a weaker witness of Christ, or being less ardent in their commitment to the truth; no one was more committed than Nephi. More empathy and less judgment of those among the rising generation who wrestle with questions would bless us all.

When they are troubled by unanswered or unanswerable questions, we can help them look to the Old Testament character, Job, whose experience mirrors life for many of us. To begin with, Job has a very comfortable life. Perhaps he is a 'Lehi.' Life is good. God blesses him. What is there to question? But then his life changes catastrophically. Job becomes a Nephi, searching for explanations.

136 John 17:3

When our young people can't get answers to their deepest, sincerest questions, their outlook on life and spiritual matters changes. The phrase 'faith crisis' has become part of our church vocabulary. I don't like it. It immediately labels searching as a disaster of spiritually, life-threatening proportions, an unexpected derailment based on the idea that 'faith' is understood with a few scriptures. But this mortal existence was never meant to be easy.

Having profound questions about what they believe is not a faith *crisis,* rather questions are a key part of their faith *journey*, or their faith *adventure.* After all, the record implies that Lehi spends a lot more time getting to the tree than standing under it.

In Job's story, his wife's reaction is quite extreme. "Curse God, and die."[137] Sometimes the rising generation may want to react that way too, especially when they don't feel proud of or sustained by their faith. They need to know that if they can't immediately resolve their struggle, they don't have to turn away from God. Once again, 'All-in' or 'all-out' are not the only two options. Remember the shelves. They don't have to let the shelf break. They can move it, replace it, and even upgrade it. By connecting to Him and trusting Him - like Lehi - they can seek His healing and find His mercy.

In the story of Job, some of his friends only have old answers to Job's new questions. They basically tell Job to stop looking; 'the answers are right in front of you, just change your attitude and be a Lehi.' This is not what he needs and not what the rising generation need either.

Job knows he has tasted the fruit. Despite finding himself in a dark and dreary wilderness, he symbolically opts to follow the man dressed in white through 'many hours of darkness'. He searches for the field and the tree. It is surely deeply symbolic and significant that almost at the very heart of the Book of Job, in chapter 19 of 42, he bears his testimony of the Saviour. "For I know that my redeemer liveth, and that he shall stand at the latter day upon the earth: And though after my skin worms destroy this body, yet in my flesh shall I see God." He knows that he has tasted the love of God before his challenges, and he holds on to that.

---

137 Job 2:9

God doesn't give him the answers he wants, but he does lead him back to the tree.

Whether our young people identify more with Nephi or Lehi, whether they struggle with questions or not, teaching them that tasting the fruit will sustain them on their adventure is essential.

While searching for their answers, they can seek opportunities to taste of the love of God through prayer, through repenting, through studying, through serving, through temple attendance, and ultimately through coming unto Christ.

We can say to those who question and to those who do not at this time, but may in the future, God knows who they are and how they struggle. He will consecrate their struggles.

He will lead them to the tree.

Teaching the rising generation to acknowledge the faith they have and to feel proud of it is an important step to learning to love the covenant path that will eventually lead them to Jesus Christ. Similarly, reassuring their acceptance of their starting points and their circumstances will create more space for them to grow in confidence and feel that they belong. Because they do.

Remember, becoming perfected (ultimately healed, restored, and made whole) in Christ is the distant end-game, the ultimate destination, a long time from now. Helping reassure our young people that they don't have to get there with an unnatural and unsustainable urgency, that in the Church they will find the eternal supports of the kingdom of God that will bind them to Him is an exciting opportunity for us all.

Chapter Summary

In order to reassure our young people that faith in Christ is something to cherish, it needs to feel authentic, personal, and fortifying.

Helping the rising generation to feel proud of the faith they have needs to be a greater focus on our local levels. Ensuring that they are not embarrassed or unsettled by the faith they don't have, or don't yet have is an area where local leaders can help. This is more true today than ever before given the global diversity within the Church.

Conclusion

I must admit, I often think about practising my faith again. The problem is that my life is in a different place today. I'm just not sure I can make the necessary changes.

Paul, 26

SERVING TOGETHER WITH JEN AS FSY SESSION DIRECTORS IN LONDON was a thrilling and healing experience for us both. Everybody has their own pandemic stories. Working alongside a uniquely gifted group of young adults and administrators allowed us to learn more about the needs of the rising generation and taught us how ready they are to lead us forward in matters of faith and inspiration. Young adults (single and married) leading, teaching, and inspiring the youth to follow Jesus Christ and seek His healing is the magic of the FSY environment. Making use of this new global programme to create a safe and validating space for our young people, an environment where they can grow their personal connections to Christ is an exciting opportunity. But FSY is just a programme, even when modernised and intentionally attuned to local sensitivities. Figuring out how to cut the ends off that faith-filled week and broaden the experience of coming unto and connecting to Christ, as opposed to a feast and famine model in between annual sessions, is an important challenge for leaders and parents to work through together.

Youth, young adults, parents, and leaders noted the change in tone and emphasis during the FSY session we directed. Stories of young people experiencing God for the first time and feeling safe enough to experiment upon the word abounded. Young people who were ready to walk away gave their church experience *one last chance* and found connection for the first time. Their stories were writ large across the letters, calls, emails, and messages we received after the experience. Families felt that a local path towards modern-day discipleship had been found, and they were excited to explore the space more intentionally.

Allow me to share a story from the life of a close friend and inspirational leader. She is a mighty woman of faith. When she teaches, I feel connected to myself and connected to my Saviour. She is kind, generous, self-deprecating and, most importantly, authentic. She has served in all manner of callings that lift the hands that hang down. She would also strongly disagree with such tributes. Her story reminds me of what people can do when they are afforded space. Let's call her Abigail.

Abigail was raised in the Church, through the Primary and Young Women organisations. Her faith in God was important to her. However, following a sudden and tragic bereavement, her family stopped attending when she had just turned seventeen. For almost a decade she wandered, close to her faith but distant from the Church. During those years, she fell in love, got married and started a family. As an anxious first-time mother, whilst pregnant, she would pray that if the Lord would deliver her baby safely, she would bring him to church (although her reconnecting with the practice of her faith was not part of her promise).

During that time, a knock at the door introduced two young missionaries. As she invited them in, Abigail felt a reassuringly familiar spirit enter her home and her heart. But the truth was that reigniting her testimony of the restored gospel and admitting to herself that she should be practising her faith was an inconvenience. Her life was now in a very different place.

As the missionaries taught her and as their bond with her family strengthened, they invited her to return to church. Her response, however, was "Sorry, I can't. When I'm with my friends, we love to drink wine and we have a great time together. I'm just not ready to give that up. It's what connects us as a group and what connects me to them."

Thinking that would be the end of it, their response startled her. These two wise, young missionaries said, in effect: "Don't worry about that. You don't have to give up wine to come to church. Just come and belong." In essence, they said "Come as you are; that is good enough right now. There aren't any rules for you to come through the chapel doors." So, she did.

Week after week she attended church. As her spiritual momentum built, Abigail noticed that she was being changed by the spirit she felt. Before long, she wanted to do all she could to please her Heavenly Father and receive His greatest blessings. She was slowly being sanctified by the Holy Ghost and began to feel healed from her wounds. In time, feeling that the Lord was again in her life and at her side, she made the necessary commitments to be recommended to the temple and never looked back.

Today, Abigail feels that had the missionaries led with an "all-in" press from the start, seeking to remind, teach, and persuade her to make temple-ready changes on day-one, she would have eventually thanked them for their time and drifted away from the regular schedule of appointments. She just wasn't ready. By trusting His loving nature and finding her own path to the healing power of Jesus Christ, Abigail found her motivation to move forward. In time, she was sealed to her family in the temple and has since become a light to all whose lives she touches.

And, yes, she did keep all her friends. They love her, and she loves them. Their friendship is built on so much more than a fine bottle of red.

The rising generation need to be reassured that being made whole in Christ is the distant end-game and not the day-one requirement. Helping them to grow confident in their faith, a faith they can feel proud of and sustained by, is one of the main purposes of the Church to which they belong.

As leaders, teachers, and parents, we can create space for our young people and their journeys of faith. Helping them to start where they are, come as they are, connect to the Source, and cast a more inclusive light on the doctrines of Christ will encourage them to feel more confident facing what lies ahead. It is my view that these tonal adjustments will enable the rising generation to travel with more authenticity for years to come. I also believe that these adjustments will help them to feel that this space is *their* church and not just that of their parents.

It's okay to change things that we've held on to for a long time. It's okay to re-evaluate our traditions, preconceptions, and prejudices. It's okay to help create a space for the rising generation to learn to love God on their terms and not ours.

We still need to lead, teach, and parent. Relying on the old rulebook has unsurprisingly not been a successful strategy for inspiring many of our young people to come unto Christ. Aligning ourselves to core doctrine, removing some of the cultural entanglements, and creating space for them to find their path to Him is an exciting way forward. The Church emphasises this in For the Strength of Youth: A Guide to Making Choices. One-size-fits-all is just not the way.

In the pre-internet world, the Church as the kingdom of God on the earth was a highly centralised (largely in the Western United States) organisation in which a generation that valued duty were happy to be led in a culture of certainty. Generational cohorts develop different values and often choose to disregard their parents' values in an effort to validate their desire for space to live according to their own. We all did it, just as the rising generation are trying to do it now.

So let's choose to help them.

Epilogue

I'm trying to find my own path through the standards. It's helpful to me when I speak with my parents to get a steer from them. They've really helped me find what works for me and what doesn't.

David, 17

An open letter to the rising generation and our friends:

Dear Friends,

In the final few verses of the Book of Mormon, Moroni concludes his writings by extending a powerful invitation to all of his eventual readers with notable generosity. He writes:

> Yea, come unto Christ, and be perfected in him, and deny yourselves of all ungodliness; and if ye shall deny yourselves of all ungodliness, and love God with all your might, mind and strength, then is his grace sufficient for you, that by his grace ye may be perfect in Christ.[138]

Of all the things he could have said, he chose to lovingly remind us that, as we deny ourselves of ungodliness, it is *our* love for God that unlocks the grace of Jesus Christ sufficient to heal us and make us whole. Deliberate in his teachings, he made the decision not to create a culture of template expectations or remind us of a prescriptive, rules-

138 Moroni 10:32

based approach. By so doing, he created space for the diversity of our circumstances, our connections, our uncertainties, our families, and our faith in Jesus Christ, so that we could "follow Him in higher and holier ways."[139]

Echoing Moroni's approach, I invite you to come unto Christ as you are and to love Him in the best way you know how. He will bless you and reassure you. Just come. You are so needed. Becoming perfected (being healed, restored, and made whole) in Him is the destination of our journey, not the departure point. Just come and belong, warts and all. Let the Lord heal you and over time sanctify you. His divine pattern to leading you safely home is, and always was, line upon line.[140] You don't have to be perfect to begin your journey or to feel connected to Him.

As you experience personal growth working with those commissioned to help you, they will lovingly lead you to covenants, ordinances, and the temple, through which you can bind yourself to Jesus Christ. The kingdom of God is where *you* belong.

Elder D. Todd Christofferson of the Quorum of the Twelve Apostles said:

> The doctrine of belonging comes down to this – each one of us can affirm: Jesus Christ died for me; He thought me worthy of His blood. He loves me and can make all the difference in my life. As I repent, His grace will transform me. I am one with Him in the gospel covenant; I belong in His Church and kingdom; and I belong in His cause to bring redemption to all of God's children.

Living the gospel of Jesus Christ is not a passive experience. But your activity doesn't need to come from a place of compliance, coercion, or conformity. I hope it can come from a place of connection, compassion, and a sense of community. There is indeed a work to do, but it's not to match up or catch up to the expectations of others. In fact, the opposite is true. We are stronger when you come as you are

139 Dieter F. Uchtdorf, *Jesus Christ Is the Strength of Youth*, General Conference (Salt Lake City: The Church of Jesus Christ of Latter-day Saints, October 2022), Gospel Library App.

140 Doctrine and Covenants 98:12

and fill this space with your light, your gifts, your talents, and your unique faith in Him.

Remember that #comeasyouare is not #dowhatyouwant or #noneofthismatters or even #therearenostandards. It's important not to misunderstand the generous invitation, no matter where you are on your journey of faith. It will always be important to safeguard and protect against rebellion. "Wickedness never was happiness."[141] And it never will be. It brings consequences that your parents, leaders, and teachers are trying to help you avoid. Their efforts and love come as boundaries and rules to guide your understanding and life. They are to keep you safe.

When everybody comes as they are, focusing on their relationships with God and one another, our shared church experience will become much more authentic and joyful with people feeling free to choose to balance personal comfort and personal growth.

Within the Church, there is already a growing culture refocusing on coming unto Christ. I invite you to look out for that and lean into it. Consider your next ordinance and prayerfully connect to the Source, seeking personal revelation regarding the choices you should make and the form your personal preparation should take. If you so desire, speak with your Bishop and ask for his help. He will want to help you. Perhaps your next ordinance is your patriarchal blessing, perhaps it is to prepare for the temple and to serve a mission. Perhaps it is to repent and prepare to take the sacrament.

Elder Uchtdorf taught:

> To be very clear, the best guide you can possibly have for making choices is Jesus Christ. . . . The purpose of *For the Strength of Youth* is to point you to Him. It teaches you eternal truths of His restored gospel—truths about who you are, who He is, and what you can accomplish with His strength. It teaches you how to make righteous choices based on those eternal truths. It's also important to know what *For the Strength of Youth* does not do. It doesn't give you a "yes" or "no" about every choice you might ever face. *For the Strength of Youth* focuses on

141 Alma 41:10

> the foundation of your choices. It focuses on values, principles, and doctrine instead of every specific behavior.[142]

If people around you respond to new opportunities to refocus on Jesus Christ by clamping down harder on the attitudes and behaviours of older paradigms, perhaps because that's where they feel most in control, they will miss the opportunity to advance.

As you advance, hopefully you will start to feel that you have more space. If you don't, please reach out to those you trust the most. There is space for you. Christ has promised that.

Being intentional, thoughtful, and prayerful while seeking His input through revelation from the Holy Ghost and getting your own response from the Lord are fundamental. Choosing to come unto Him as you are and connecting to Him will help you. Speaking with your friends and your family will help you.

Here is one final example. In the UK, films with more grown-up content are rated either certificate 15 or 18, denoting how old you need to be to watch them in the cinema. All films that are rated 15 or 18 are rated R in the US. There is no similar sub-division of the R-rated movie classification, splitting mid-teens from adults. As an LDS family in the UK, we knew very well what the Church culture and the *For the Strength of Youth* standards taught about R-rated films. But it never felt relevant to us.

We never spent any time working out what films released in the UK were R-rated and which were not. As a family, we discussed what felt appropriate and what didn't. We made informed and intentional choices based on genre, content, tone, and entertainment value. Sometimes we got it wrong, but mostly we got it right. Mum and Dad gave their inputs and advice. Then they gave us space to make our own choices. Together we decided to avoid 15— and 18— rated movies generally but chose to carve out 'historically-themed' action movies depicting war and the more violent chapters of history. As a family, we loved the film Gladiator (2000). In the UK it was rated certificate 15.

---

142 Dieter F. Uchtdorf, *Jesus Christ Is the Strength of Youth*, General Conference (Salt Lake City: The Church of Jesus Christ of Latter-day Saints, October 2022), Gospel Library App.

I was set apart as a missionary on the evening of Christmas Day 2000, after having spent the afternoon watching Gladiator. My favourite line "what we do in life, echoes in eternity," to me felt poignant as I flew out to the Provo MTC the next morning.

On the first Sunday, during our first sacrament meeting as a zone, we were invited to bear our testimonies. I chose to stand and, in front of a very large group of Utah missionaries, referenced Gladiator as my favourite movie. I shared the above quote (cue awkward gasps), linked it to my mission, bore a simple testimony of the Saviour, and sat down.

At the end of the testimony meeting, a leader took me to one side. He reprimanded me for how inappropriate my testimony had been and told me that I should think more carefully next time before lowering the tone of the meeting. I genuinely had no idea what he was referring to.

Later, my companion, whilst laughing uncontrollably told me that Gladiator was rated R in the US. "Only Norton would quote an R-rated movie his first time bearing his testimony at the MTC."

The point? Try and avoid letting others (however well-intentioned) prescribe your interpretation of the Lord's standards. They can give advice, and you would certainly do well to listen to good advice. But if you let others make decisions for you, their overwhelming influence will rob you of the great opportunity you have to form your own personal connection to the Source and feel led by the Spirit to your own conclusions. You will form rich learning opportunities and lasting righteous habits as you seek guidance from God and make an intentional choice. This is why God gave you agency, to invite you to learn and grow with Him as He guides you. As you trust Him, He will always be your guide and your support.

As you seek your own path to Him through your best efforts, covenants, and ordinances, you will find confidence in your faith. Acknowledge that you will make mistakes, have to reset, repent, and go again. This is part of coming unto Christ. Remember, being perfected, healed, restored, and made whole in Him takes an eternal lifetime, not just a mortal one.

We are right to dress appropriately in a way that values who we are and whose we are. It is right to use soft language and avoid media that is harmful to our souls. But you get to choose your own path to Him as you are led by the influence of the Holy Ghost. Church is an imperfect space for you to test your learnings, renew your covenants, and receive your ordinances.

Be grateful for a living prophet who is turning pages and inviting us to focus on coming unto Christ. As we become intentional about that invitation, we will find strength in converting our desires into faith and our faith into knowledge. In that safe space, which we need you to help us build, gathering people of every place and from every place, we hope that you will feel that you belong. We know you will help others to feel the same way.

The starting point is #comeasyouare, but there is so much more that follows it. With more space afforded to you by your leaders, teachers, and parents, it's now time to put the *rise* into rising generation. We need *all of you*. We need you to lead us forward. We need you to show us the way to a more radically inclusive space that enables everybody to come unto Jesus Christ, be healed, be restored, and return safely home. Take the opportunities that come from the space that is being created. Rise up. Connect to Him. Search the Scriptures. Follow the promptings that come from the Holy Ghost. Walk *your* path with conviction alongside those you love. Be patient with those that love you and with those that are learning to love you. Be patient with yourselves. Help them help you. Show us what you are made of. Do what you were sent here to do. Become who you are destined to become, and lead us to that promised land.

With love and admiration,
Sam

To those who wander,

Nobody truly knows your story. Nobody can ever truly know your history, your challenges, or your traumas. Equally, nobody knows your deep desires, hopes, your dreams, or your ambitions. Nobody sees what you've had to deal with in your life, or what you are currently dealing with.

But He does.

As we try and pursue a more determined #comeasyouare mindset in welcoming people, as we strive to connect people to the Source and not just to the Church, or to a sense of duty or habit, or to just their callings, as we broaden the vocabulary and remove as many loaded labels and mindsets as we can, as we share a more inclusive version of Heavenly Father's plan and focus ourselves on the merits, mercy, and healing of the Atonement of Jesus Christ, we will get better at creating a safe space where people may choose to return. If you one day choose to do the same, we'll all be stronger for it. As you continue to wander, perhaps remember this revelation from God, penned by one of the ultimate wilderness wanderers:

> And I will also be your light in the wilderness; and I will prepare the way before you, if it so be that ye shall keep my commandments; wherefore, inasmuch as ye shall keep my commandments ye shall be led towards the promised land; and ye shall know that it is by me that ye are led.[143]

With my love and respect,
Jen

143 1 Nephi 17:13

Notes

Notes

Notes

Notes

Notes

Notes

Notes

Notes

About the Author

Sam and Jen are British members of the Church, born and raised in the United Kingdom. Sam has spent the last 18 years working with the youth of the Church, including as a Bishop in London, and having served as Stake Young Men's president for four years and in the stake presidency for eight years. He is currently serving as a seminary teacher and works in banking and finance. Jen is a paediatric nurse and most recently served as ward Relief Society president, as well as various callings in the Young Women and Primary organisations. Sam and Jen have been married for 19 years and have four children. They recently served together as FSY Session Directors for London from 2021 to 2023.

cayasayhello@gmail.com

Scan the QR code to see the
Come as You Are Insatgram account